MW00787071

Careers in Child and Adolescent Development

Child and adolescent development is a rich and continuously evolving field that offers a wealth of career opportunities. *Careers in Child and Adolescent Development* is the first textbook to guide students along each step of the career path—from the levels of academic degrees and programs available, to preparations for the professional world. It presents a brief description of the field, explores a broad array of career paths available to students, and offers some practical ideas for constructing a career plan. Students are provided with practical, up-to-date information about career opportunities, combined with real-life vignettes to illustrate the challenges and rewards these careers hold. The book presents traditional career paths in fields such as early childhood education, elementary education, educational leadership, and school counseling, as well as non-traditional or emerging career paths in child life and behavior analysis, research, academia, nonprofit work, children's ministry, and family law. It will serve as a go-to reference for students, and can be used in a fieldwork class, a service learning class, a professional development class, or a capstone class.

Kimberly A. Gordon Biddle has a PhD from Stanford University in child and adolescent development. She is an American Psychological Association MFP Fellow. She is a college professor of 26 years who currently works at California State University, Sacramento. This is her second co-authored textbook. She is the author or co-author of more than 15 peer-reviewed articles and some book chapters. She is a presenter or co-presenter of more than 35 peer-reviewed presentations. Kimberly was the recipient of a Stanford GSE Alumni Award for Excellence in Education for 2018.

Aletha M. Harven is an assistant professor of Psychology and Child Development at California State University, Stanislaus. She obtained her BA and MA at Sacramento State University and her PhD from the University of California, Los Angeles. She has authored and co-authored book chapters, peer-reviewed articles, and peer-reviewed presentations.

Cynthia Hudley is a professor emerita in the Department of Education Educational Psychology program at the University of California, Santa Barbara. She also served as an associate dean for the University of California, Santa Barbara Graduate Division, president of Division E of the American Educational Research Association, and a member of the Board of Educational Affairs for the American Psychological Association.

Careers in Child and Adolescent Development

A Student's Guide to Working in the Field

Kimberly A. Gordon Biddle,
Aletha M. Harven, and Cynthia Hudley

Routledge
Taylor & Francis Group

NEW YORK AND LONDON

First published 2018
by Routledge
711 Third Avenue, New York, NY 10017

and by Routledge
2 Park Square, Milton Park, Abingdon, Oxon, OX14 4RN

Routledge is an imprint of the Taylor & Francis Group, an informa business

© 2018 Taylor & Francis

The right of Kimberly A. Gordon Biddle, Aletha M. Harven, and
Cynthia Hudley to be identified as authors of this work has been
asserted by them in accordance with sections 77 and 78 of the
Copyright, Designs and Patents Act 1988.

All rights reserved. No part of this book may be reprinted or
reproduced or utilised in any form or by any electronic, mechanical,
or other means, now known or hereafter invented, including
photocopying and recording, or in any information storage or
retrieval system, without permission in writing from the publishers.

Trademark notice: Product or corporate names may be trademarks
or registered trademarks, and are used only for identification and
explanation without intent to infringe.

Library of Congress Cataloging-in-Publication Data
Names: Gordon, Kimberly A. (Kimberly Ann), 1965– author. | Harven,
   Aletha M., author. | Hudley, Cynthia, author.
Title: Careers in child and adolescent development : a student's
   guide to working in the field / Kimberly A. Gordon Biddle,
   Aletha M. Harven, and Cynthia Hudle.
Description: New York, NY : Routledge, 2018. | Includes bibliographical
   references and index.
Identifiers: LCCN 2017056365 | ISBN 9781138859968 (hbk : alk. paper) |
   ISBN 9781138859951 (pbk : alk. paper) | ISBN 9780203705216 (ebk)
Subjects: LCSH: Child development—Vocational guidance. |
   Adolescent development—Vocational guidance.
Classification: LCC HQ767.85 .G67 2018 | DDC 305.231023—dc23
LC record available at https://lccn.loc.gov/2017056365

ISBN: 978-1-138-85996-8 (hbk)
ISBN: 978-1-138-85995-1 (pbk)
ISBN: 978-0-203-70521-6 (ebk)

Typeset in Sabon
by Apex CoVantage, LLC

Kimberly—This book is dedicated to God without whom this book would not be possible. It is also dedicated to my mother, Mary, and my brother, Randy, because they inspire me. They are my beginnings. Most importantly, this book is dedicated to my husband, Chris, and my son, Manny. They are my present and my future. They not only inspire me, they assist me and motivate me. Without them this book would not be possible, either. I love them and they love me. I am forever grateful for their love and support, as this book would not have been completed without them.

Aletha—I'd like to thank my family and friends for their continued support in all of my academic endeavors. It's exciting to have contributed to a book that will assist people in their pursuit of a meaningful career within the field of child and adolescent development.

Cynthia—to my husband, James, who reminds me what matters.

Contents

Preface   xiv
Foreword by Amado M. Padilla   xv

PART 1
Getting Started   1

1 The Field of Child and Adolescent Development   3

Past, Present, and Future 3
  Past State of the Field 3
  Present State of the Field 4
  Future Directions for the Field 6
Application of Developmental Theories 8
Degrees, Careers, and Other Related Fields 8
Outline for the Remainder of the Book 9
Reflective Questions 9
References 10

2 Examining Career Theory and Metaphors   11

Overview of Career Theory 11
Some Theoretical Perspectives on Careers 12
Career Metaphors 14
Summary 17
Reflective Questions 17
References 17

PART 2
Careers   19

3 Careers in ECE (Birth to Third Grade)   21

Child and Adolescent Development as a Foundation 21
Possible Jobs in ECE 22
Early Head Start and Head Start: Federal ECE Positions 26

Career Paths in ECE 27
  Alice's Interview 27
  Jean's Interview 28
  Annette's Interview 29
Career Specifics 30
  Salary 30
  Ethics 31
Summary 31
Reflective Questions 32
Is This Right for You? 32
References 32

4   Careers in Middle Elementary Through Adult Education   **34**

Human Development for Teachers 34
A Brief Primer on Concepts Important for Teachers 35
  Milestones 35
  Tasks 35
  Strengths and Barriers 36
Overview of Job Types 37
  Public Schools 38
  Private Schools 39
Teacher Certification 39
  Alternative Teacher Certification 40
Why Teaching? 40
  Mrs. Johnson's Interview 41
Career Specifics 41
  Personal Characteristics 42
  Professional Characteristics 43
  Diversity 44
  Social Justice 45
  Ethics 45
Summary 46
Reflective Questions 46
Is This Right for You? 46
References 46

5   Educational Leaders and Educational Agencies: Pre-K Through 12th Grade   **48**

Careers With School Districts 48
  Mallory's Interview 49
  Stan's Interview 50
  The General Path 50
Governmental Offices of Education 50
  Nora's Interview 51

Career Specifics 52
   Characteristics and Abilities 52
   Salary 52
   Ethics 53
Summary 55
Reflective Questions 55
Is This Right for You? 55
References 55

6 Educational Consultants and Specialists   **57**

Requirements and Duties as Explained in Literature 57
   Education and Experience Needed 58
   Settings and Duties 59
Real-Life Interviews 59
   Vanessa's Interview 59
   Ralph's Interview 61
Career Specifics 62
   Characteristics and Abilities 62
   Risks 62
   Salary 62
   Ethics 62
Summary 63
Reflective Questions 63
Is This Right for You? 63
References 64

7 College and University Positions: Teaching, Researching, Leading, and Providing Service   **65**

Preparing for College and University Positions 66
   Community Colleges 67
   Four-Year, Public Universities and Colleges 68
   Private, Nonprofit Colleges and Universities 70
   Leadership Positions in Colleges and Universities 71
Career Specifics 72
   Ethics 72
   Salary 72
Summary 74
Reflective Questions 74
Is This Right for You? 75
References 75

8 Nonprofit Organizations   **76**

Nonprofit Positions and Careers 76
   Volunteers 76

Committee Members 77
Board of Directors 77
Executive Director or CEO 77
Development Staff 77
Advisory Board 77
Familiar Nonprofit Organizations 78
American Heart Association 78
March of Dimes 78
Children's Defense Fund 78
Make-A-Wish 79
Desired Knowledge, Skills, and Abilities 79
Cultural Competence 79
Self-Starter (Self-Directed) 80
Data Savvy 80
Design Thinking 80
Collaborative Spirit 80
Strong Work Ethic and Ability to Work Long Hours 80
Innovation 81
Time Management Skills 81
Adaptability 81
Recommended Practices 81
Interview With Aisha Lowe, PhD 82
Why a Nonprofit? 82
Nonprofit Work 83
Beneficial Skills 83
Career Specifics 84
Salary 84
Summary 84
Reflective Questions 84
Is This Right for You? 84
References 84

9 Counseling and School Psychology   **86**

Career Counselors 86
Description and Preparation 86
Duties and Workplace Settings 86
Marriage, Family, and Child Counselors 87
Description and Training 87
Duties and Settings 87
School Counselors 87
General Description, Training, Duties, and Settings 87
Kerrie's Interview 87
School Psychologists 88
Description and Preparation 88

Daily Duties and Work Settings 89
Sam's Interview 89
Career Specifics 90
Ethics 90
Salary 91
Summary 91
Reflective Questions 92
Is This Right for You? 92
References 92

10 Behavior Analyst   94

Needed Characteristics and Abilities 94
Settings for Positions 95
Obtaining Board Certification 95
Real-Life Interviews 97
Cherie's Interview 97
Kristina's Interview 98
Career Specifics 99
Ethics 99
Salary 99
Summary 99
Reflective Questions 99
Is This Right for You? 100
References 100

11 Child Life Specialist and Other Health Careers   101

Requirements for Becoming a Child Life Specialist 101
Current Requirements 101
Future Requirements 103
Duties of a Child Life Specialist 104
Real-Life Interviews 104
Angel's Interview 104
Erin's Interview 105
Desirable Personal Characteristics 106
Workplace Settings 106
Career Specifics 106
Ethics 106
Salary 106
Other Health Professions 107
Summary 107
Reflective Questions 107
Is This Right for You? 108
References 108

12 Other Career Possibilities   **109**

Nanny 109
Children's Ministry 110
  Frank's Interview 110
Family Lawyer 111
Juvenile Justice 112
Adoption Caseworker 112
Foster Care Parent 112
Nonlicensed Social Work 113
Museum Positions 113
  Gary's Interview 114
Recreational Therapy 115
Occupational Therapy 115
Children's Librarian 115
  Sally's Interview 116
Summary 116
Reflective Questions 117
Is This Right for You? 117
References 117

PART 3
Discovering Your Path   **119**

13 Reflections on Self   **121**

Reflecting on Yourself and Your Current Situation 121
  Self-Reflection 121
  Current Situation 123
  A Summary of Resources 124
  The Process 125
Determining Your Goals and Plans 126
  Career Goals 126
  Personal Goals 127
Standard Career Assessment Tools 127
  Myers Briggs Type Inventory 128
  The Personalities 128
  Strong Interest Inventory Assessment 128
  Campbell Interest and Skill Inventory 129
  Career Beliefs Inventory 129
  The Career Key Test 132
After Reflecting and Assessing 132
  Becoming a Professional 133
  The Foundation 133

Summary 133
Reflective Questions 134
References 134

14 Reflections on Career Preparation   **135**

Job Search Process and Tools 135
  Job Search Tools 135
Gaining Pre-Employment Experience 139
Social Media Presence 139
General Job Ethics 140
Summary 140
Reflective Questions 140
References 140

Index   **141**

Preface

This book came to be because of two trends that I recognized in my daily life. One trend was the growth of, definition of, importance of, and increased interest in the field of child and adolescent development. The other trend was a number of students coming to me for advice about what careers were available to them in the field of child and adolescent development once they graduated. Since I graduated from Stanford University Graduate School of Education in 1993 with a PhD in child and adolescent development, I (Kimberly A. Gordon Biddle) have seen the field grow in terms of reputation and numbers of students. I really want to help students to see the variety of positions available to them with this field as their base. I also want the world to know that we prepare more than just early childhood educators. Child and adolescent development is a good foundation for K–12 teachers, counselors of various types, and nonprofit organizations, children's ministers, and other related professions. I want people to know. Quite simply, that is how I began on a journey to write this book. Upon publication of this book, more people will know and I will have accomplished my goal.

Acknowledgements

We want to acknowledge Sadat Zarek, Lindsey Pitts, Veronika Kolesnikov, and Annya Dahmani who provided research and administrative assistance.

Foreword

Today educators and policy makers spend considerable time and resources in planning and implementing high school programs directed at making college readiness a reality for all students. The focus of these programs is to provide students with the necessary information and academic skills they will need to transition to college and be competitive in higher education. In some school districts, attention is also given to workplace readiness: The focus is on employer requirements and what skills and mastery level the high school graduate needs in order to find secure employment that will offer economic stability and well-being in the years ahead. However, when students transition out of high school to either a two-year or four-year college they often experience a void in what they can expect in the way of employment in their chosen field of study. Many students find the college to career track bewildering, filled with false starts and with little guidance for next steps into the world of job searches, job applications, and getting hired.

This book is intended to fill the void for college students pursuing a program in child and adolescent development. Students naturally want to know what career options are available to them, and many students want some guidance on career options before they go too far down the road in selecting a major field of study. It's my experience that as university faculty we do a very poor job of mentoring our students in the career pathways available to them once they complete their academic program. We typically excel at presenting the important information about developmental theories and research that supports these theories in our classrooms, but we typically fail in showing the relevance of these theories and research to the actual day-to-day practice of caring and instructing children in real-life contexts where children are found and where there is a need for well-trained professionals knowledgeable of developmental processes and the intricacies of best practices in working with families and children.

In this book Kimberly Gordon Biddle, Aletha Harven, and Cynthia Hudley translate their deep knowledge of and passion for child and adolescent development into a set of very practical guidelines for students in an effort to facilitate students' entry into a suitable career pathway. In this handy and yet scholarly book the authors go the extra mile to show students that there are a multitude of careers available in the field of child development. In very carefully crafted language that is suitable for community college students, university level undergraduate students, or graduate students, Biddle and company map out the various career trajectories available to students with differing levels of academic preparation—associate of arts, bachelor of arts, or graduate degree. They also ask the readers throughout to reflect on their career goals and types of employment opportunities that they might find rewarding.

With approximately 75 million children under the age of 18 today, and with our increasingly diverse population of children, working parents, absence of extended family members to provide child care, and increasing array of public and private early child education programs, afterschool programs of different types, and child specialists in health and non-profit organizations engaged in work with children and families there is greater need now more than ever to have a well-trained professional workforce in the child care–related fields. However, these new professionals need mentoring and guidance at the entry stage to their career and this is where the utility of this book comes in. The book will be a welcome addition to a broad array of educators tasked with the training of new professionals in child and adolescent development and an important reference book for students.

We all can agree that there is no work more important than the caring and education of our children. The authors of this book are to be congratulated for the wisdom and guidance they provide students wishing to enter this most noble profession. It's important to know that there are numerous pathways for individuals who want to work with children and this book provides the roadmap into the profession.

Lastly, everyone in the ever-expanding field of child and adolescent development and in the multitude of programs serving our children owe Kimberly Gordon Biddle, Aletha Harven, and Cynthia Hudley a debt of gratitude for authoring this book because while it is intended for students, it will serve as a reference guide for a broad spectrum of faculty members and career counselors, all of whom in some way are involved in guiding the next generation of professionals in exciting careers in child and adolescent development.

Amado M. Padilla
Professor and Chair
Developmental and Psychological Sciences
Graduate School of Education
Stanford University

Part 1

Getting Started

Chapter 1

The Field of Child and Adolescent Development

To successfully work within the field of child and adolescent development, educators must understand the ways in which humans develop cognitively, socially, emotionally, and physically across the lifespan. Therefore, effective professionals must understand the *principles of development* (e.g., development is orderly and cumulative), the *domains* in which development occurs (e.g., cognitive, social, emotional, and physical), the *interrelated nature* of the domains (e.g., social interactions influence cognitive growth), the *developmental periods* (e.g., toddlerhood, early childhood, adolescence), the *factors influencing development* across the domains (e.g., heredity), and the *contexts* in which development takes place (e.g., home, school, peer groups). It is equally important for educators to understand both developmental and educational theories of children's development and learning, so as to cultivate the skills to effectively engage youth in developmentally appropriate practices. By acquiring a solid understanding of children and their development, educators should be able to effectively (a) identify and address the unique needs of diverse children and adolescents; (b) engage youth in curricular activities that speak to their individual needs; and (c) assist caregivers and other educators in promoting the healthy development of all youth. The purpose of this introductory chapter is to provide a lens for current and prospective educators to better understand the field of child and adolescent development, from its history and theoretical frameworks to the exciting careers associated with this field of study.

Past, Present, and Future

Past State of the Field

The field of child and adolescent development has evolved over time due to shifting societal views of children. Prior to the 19th and 20th centuries, most societies treated children like small adults, where they are given great responsibility and expected to fully contribute to family and community life. It was not uncommon for children, particularly in rural communities, to work alongside their caregivers during the day, assist with cooking meals for their families, and to provide care for their siblings. Also not uncommon was children's exposure to sexual play and exploitation—and work within the labor market (Lowe, 2009). Children were not seen as having rights and were often exposed to various forms of abuse at a very early age (Lowe, 2009). School attendance did not become mandatory until compulsory education laws were enacted, which required children to attend school from early childhood through late adolescence. These laws were enacted to increase literacy rates and to protect children from child labor practices. In the United States, Massachusetts in 1852 was the first state to enact a compulsory education law, while in 1917 Mississippi was the last state to enact a compulsory education law. These education laws helped pave the way for a more educated society and an increase in high-level jobs outside of the home environment.

Noteworthy is how the` idea of "childhood" became recognized as a stage separate from that of "adulthood" between the 13th century and modern times, but it was during the early modern period (17th century) that the term "childhood" began to take on some of its modern meanings, particularly among the middle class (Lowe, 2009). And by the 18th century, the term was acknowledged as a valuable stage to be explored (Lowe, 2009). This societal shift in thinking was important in moving beyond viewing children as small adults and laborers to viewing children as innocent young people, whose needs were separate from that of adults. This evolving view led to an increase in the creation of appropriate clothing, developmentally appropriate games, and other pastime activities that spoke to the needs of children (Lowe, 2009). Also unique to this shift in thinking was the emergence of laws in 1875 in the United States that were created to protect the rights of children. Additionally, there was an increase in the scholarship on children, which was inspired by the work of **William Preyer,** who founded child psychology in 1882 when he authored the book, *Die Seele des Kindes* (The Soul of the Child). Preyer also pioneered research methods such as empirical observation and experimentation for work within the field of human development, thereby laying the groundwork for the study of "childhood." Other scholars who have contributed to the field of child and adolescent development include **John Piaget,** who identified four stages of cognitive growth from birth to adolescence; **Erik Erikson,** who identified eight stages of psychosocial development across the lifespan; **John B. Watson,** who emphasized the role of social environmental factors, such as caregivers, on children's development; **Lev Vygotsky,** who focused on the link between social interactions and cognitive development; and **Albert Bandura,** who emphasized the relation between children's perceptions and their subsequent behavior and learning outcomes. In regards to understanding appropriate pedagogical practices for increasing children's overall development, many educators consult the work of **John Dewey,** whose progressive education approach emphasized the need for educational activities to be practical and relevant to children's lives. **Maria Montessori** is also renowned for her emphasis on self-correcting learning tools for aiding in children's individual learning. Further, **Loris Malaguzzi** developed the Reggio Emilia education approach, which was inspired by Italian culture and the residents of Reggio Emilia, Italy. This approach emphasizes the development of individualized curriculums that emerge from the creativity of each child. Many of the scholars mentioned here were *constructivists* who believed that children should be allowed the freedom to construct their own knowledge with guidance and collaborative efforts from adults. The work of the aforementioned scholars has helped shape societal views on children, including their development and learning. However, there is still much debate on the amount of freedom children should be given over their own learning and development, as well as on the educational tools and activities that educators should use to promote development. As educators, it is our duty to continue learning about "childhood," given the growing scholarship on children and our shifting societal values, so as to effectively guide the development and learning of all children.

Present State of the Field

Given the diversity among children and adolescents in terms of culture, race, ethnicity, gender, socioeconomic status, sexual orientation, disability status, and the like, it has been imperative for educators to understand the role that diversity plays in the lives of children and adolescents. It is well known that the developmental models utilized to assess children and adolescents are primarily based on research emphasizing the experiences of White middle-class youth. This generalized framework often leads to the negative devaluation of youth whose cultural norms differ from that of White youth. Therefore, educators must become culturally competent, so as to find value in children's cultural differences and to become comfortable with those differences in learning and development. "Cultural competence" is defined here as understanding and finding value in the cultural differences that children and their families bring to educational contexts, so as to design meaningful assessments and effective learning opportunities, and to provide appropriate support, among other activities (McAllister & Irvine, 2000). Cultural competence also includes the understanding that all children are not having the same experiences due to many factors. For instance, many African American adolescents will experience racial discrimination in school, which has been associated with poor mental health and academic functioning (Wong, Eccles, & Sameroff, 2003; Eccles, Wong, & Peck, 2006). However, African American students who possess a strong racial identity are less likely to experience the negative consequences associated with school racial discrimination (Wong, Eccles, & Sameroff, 2003; Eccles, Wong, & Peck, 2006). Thus, educators seeking to be culturally competent could use these research findings to understand the unique challenges faced by Black youth. Also, educators could increase their vigilance of discriminatory practices, explore and disrupt their own biases, and assist Black youth in developing a strong racial identity (see Harven & Soodjinda, 2016, for a discussion on social justice teaching). Another example is of an Asian American girl with a learning disability, who feels a great deal of pressure to perform well in school due to her teachers' endorsement of the model minority stereotype, which posits that Asian American students are *naturally smart*. This seemingly positive stereotype often leaves many Asian and Asian American students with a lack of academic support, while also placing them at risk for poor mental health (Lee, 1994). Thus, educators seeking to be culturally competent should challenge their stereotypes about Asian and Asian American students, so as to provide these youth with appropriate support mechanisms. A final example is of a young child who has two mothers and is teased regularly by his classmates. Educators seeking to be culturally competent should not shy away from engaging their classes in an open discussion about differing family types, so as to normalize the unique family structures of all their students. This normalization could be done through class discussions and readings on diverse family types—and engaging children in art activities to depict their family structures. Please note that being culturally competent includes being aware of children's intersecting and overlapping social identities (e.g., an *American Indian child* who is a *male soccer player*). Noteworthy is how children's intersecting identities are likely to influence their development in different ways. For instance, the educational experiences of children who are Latinx and male might differ from children who are Latinx and female, due to males of color receiving harsher forms of punishment in school (see Noguera, 2003a, for a discussion on school disciplinary practices). Also, a White male with a learning disability might receive more assistance in school than a Black male with a learning disability, due to stereotypes about the educability of Black male youth (see Noguera, 2003b and Reynolds, 2010 for a discussion on teacher bias in the classroom). Thus, it is imperative for educators to explore the diverse and intersecting identities that children bring with them to the educational context, so as to develop a basic level of cultural competence in which to understand children and provide them with equitable educational experiences.

Equally important to the field of child and adolescent development is the recognition of children's rights. The Reggio Emilia approach to early childhood education (ECE) espouses the idea that children have the *right* to learn, develop, and express themselves in many different ways across diverse sociocultural contexts (Hewett, 2001). This approach makes the distinction between *child-time* and *adult-time*, as educators should acknowledge that children have the right to learn on their own time and at their own pace, so as to process information in a meaningful way. All too often, educators are consumed with their own curricular goals—forgetting that learning objectives should emerge from the curiosity and interests of the child (Rinaldi, 1993; Hewett, 2001). That is, if while playing outdoors, children become interested in the color of the sky, teachers could create developmentally appropriate activities that assist children in making sense of the sky. Teachers could facilitate learning by inquiring about children's current knowledge of the sky; encourage children to view the sky at different times throughout the day; and encourage them to use authentic art supplies to depict the sky and its natural surroundings (e.g., coloring pencils, real grass, bark from a tree, etc.). These varied activities will support the curiosity of children, thereby helping them to make sense of their worlds. Noteworthy is how Jean Piaget felt that children were constantly moving from a state of disequilibrium (e.g., curiosity about the sky) to a state of equilibrium (e.g., understanding the colors of the sky) through the processes of assimilation (i.e., incorporating new information into existing schemes or linking new information with current knowledge) and accommodation (modifying or developing a scheme or making room for new information). Thus, child-time allows children to investigate their questions in a state of disequilibrium through observations, discussions, readings, playing, painting, drawing, coloring, and other creative activities. Therefore, educators who value children's developmental rights should allow curricular activities to emerge naturally from the child, pace curricular activities to accordance with the child's understanding of the material, and provide guidance and collaborative efforts. This pacing of curricula is not always easy given the various standards to which classroom educators must adhere, but it is important for educators to utilize developmental theory to assist children in developing knowledge to effectively function in their worlds. Also important is the recognition of caregiver rights, where educators should assist caregivers in their efforts to advocate for the equitable treatment of their children, as well as to obtain access to important educational services. For instance, caregivers who perceive their child to have a learning disability should be informed by educators on the protocol for requesting assessments and on receiving appropriate intervention services. Lastly, educators must understand and engage children in developmentally appropriate practice (DAP), which is a teaching approach grounded in research on the ways in which young children develop and learn at different stages of development (Copple & Bredekamp, 2009). Educators engaged in DAP should have knowledge of normative developmental patterns and outcomes at each age and stage of development; utilize observations of children to meet their individual needs; and make an effort to become familiar with the cultural values and expectations of children's families, so as to provide respectful and relevant experiences for children and their families (Copple & Bredekamp, 2009). Educators working with adolescents should build upon DAP by seeking research regarding appropriate practices to use with teens. In sum, it is imperative for professionals within the field of child and adolescent development to learn as much as they can about the unique lives of the children and families with whom they serve.

Future Directions for the Field

The field of child and adolescent development must continue to shift its focus toward cultural competence or the ability for educators to understand and interact with children and families from diverse cultural groups. No longer can educators afford to feel overwhelmed by the idea of learning about children's diverse cultural needs. Instead, educators should find value and joy in learning about children and their families, so as to effectively engage youth in enriching activities.

Interdisciplinary Approaches to the Study of Human Development

Educators should draw their information about children and adolescents from complimentary disciplines such as psychology, which explores human behavior including mental health; sociology, which explores the effects of societal issues on diverse populations (e.g., poverty); social work, which provides insight on how to effectively address unhealthy family dynamics; and teacher education, which provides information on impactful pedagogical practices. It is equally important for scholars within the field to engage in interdisciplinary work that further explores differing aspects of children's adjustment.

Current Issues and Events

Effective educators should understand the ways in which current issues impact children's psychological, psychosocial, and academic functioning, such as the shooting of unarmed Black males, the threat of deportation, the challenge of battling stereotypes, and various forms of harassment.

Children With Disabilities

Under the Individuals with Disability Education Act (IDEA), all children and adolescents are supposed to receive effective levels of care and support from educators and service providers. However, educators must recognize the many factors that influence the type of care that young people receive such as disability type, school type (e.g., private, public), the communities in which children reside (e.g., low income, middle income), and the extent to which educators engage in deficit thinking regarding children with disabilities and their intersecting identities. The aforementioned factors could have a negative impact on whether students with disabilities increase their cognitive, social, emotional, and physical abilities.

Mental Health

A deeper exploration of children's mental health needs is critical in understanding how home, community, and school-related factors can positively or negatively impact their psychological, psychosocial, and academic functioning.

Intersectionality in Identity Formation

As previously mentioned, educators must recognize the ways in which children's growing identities emerge and intersect to influence their diverse developmental trajectories. This understanding is helpful in accepting all children as they are.

Utilizing Technology

Creative play should incorporate not only the use of natural and authentic materials and activities but should also incorporate technology for those children whose virtual worlds are just as important as their offline worlds.

Application of Developmental Theories

Educators within the field of child and adolescent development are often called upon to utilize their knowledge of developmental principles and theories to guide children's learning and behavior, to solve problems such as peer conflict, and to guide caregivers and other educators in promoting children's healthy development. For instance, in studying *cognitive development*, educators learn how children's perceptions, thoughts, and understandings of their worlds change over time due to biological maturation, exploratory experiences, and knowledge attainment in both formal settings (e.g., at school) and informal settings (e.g., on the playground). It is imperative for educators to recognize how continual changes in children's thinking, reasoning, and understanding have a significant influence on their academic, behavioral, and psychological functioning, so as to understand children's needs at different stages of development (e.g., early childhood and early childhood versus adolescence). Related theories emphasizing children's cognitive development include the importance of culturally relevant pedagogy, which encourages educators to use their cultural knowledge to increase learning (Gloria Ladson-Billings, 1995, 2014). Paolo Freire's work on critical literacy encourages educators to honor children's unique perspectives and narratives, while also engaging them in transformative and action-oriented learning (Freire, 1996). In studying *social development*, educators begin to understand how children learn through socialization, where caregivers, siblings, friends, teachers, community members, and the like guide children in the acquisition of beliefs, values, behaviors and knowledge deemed appropriate for healthy functioning within a particular society. Books, computer programs, and the media are also social in nature and act as socializing agents for children and adolescents. Therefore, educators can utilize their understanding of socialization to guide children's development and assist caregivers in effectively interacting with their children so as to promote healthy functioning. In studying *emotional development*, educators learn how to help children identify and manage their emotions effectively. Also, by understanding the ways in which children's biologically programmed emotions (e.g., joy) and learned emotions (e.g., shame) can influence their perceptions, thoughts, behavior, and personality, educators can help children to develop healthy emotion-behavior patterns by encouraging positive patterns (e.g., interest–exploration) and disrupting negative patterns (e.g., sadness–aggression). Lastly, in studying children's *physical development*, educators learn about changes in children's bodies, physical appearance, and movement at different stages of development.

Degrees, Careers, and Other Related Fields

Educators can obtain one or more of the following degrees in child or human development, family studies, and education: Associate of Art (AA), Bachelor of Art (BA), Bachelor of Science (BS), Master of Art (MA), Master of Science (MS), Doctor of Philosophy (PhD) or Doctor of Education (EdD). Prospective professionals should explore all degree types to determine the educational path best suited for their desired career. An Associate degree will allow educators to work within the early childhood environment as a teacher or site coordinator. A Bachelor's degree and a Master's degree will allow educators to continue working within the early childhood sector. A Bachelor's degree is sufficient for entry-level positions, while advanced degrees and credentials are essential for K–12 teaching, supervisory positions, clinical and therapeutic counseling positions, and positions as program directors and coordinators. A PhD is often pursued among educators who wish to conduct research and/or teach at the university level, while those pursuing an EdD often desire to continue in leadership work (e.g., school administration). It is noteworthy that prospective educators can pursue an interdisciplinary education by combining degree programs that are closely aligned with child development, such as developmental psychology and education. Additional specializations and training qualify educators for higher positions and pay. Following are some examples of careers that prospective and current educators can pursue.

> *Child care/preschool:* Tutor or peer mentor in preschools, Head Start programs, religious organizations
> *Education:* early childhood specialist or teacher in preschool and K–12 school settings
> *Community service:* research and evaluation in hospitals; program coordinators in community centers and summer camp programs
> *Social services:* case manager, counselor, or administrator in nonprofit organizations, group homes, treatment facilities, and youth services agencies
> *Medical:* child life specialist or occupational therapist in hospitals, health care facilities, and health and wellness agencies
> *Social services:* rehabilitation or advocacy work in federal, state, and local government agencies
> *Communications:* various positions within journalism, public relations, or children's book publishing
> *Business:* positions in management, sales, or customer service in manufacturing companies of children's clothes, toys, furniture, and food

Note that there are many more careers within the field of child and adolescent development that will be explored throughout this book.

Outline for the Remainder of the Book

This book is designed to assist prospective and current educators in understanding the many careers within the field of child and adolescent development, so as to determine the career trajectory that is best suited for their needs. Following this introductory chapter is Chapter 2 on career theory and practice, Chapter 3 on careers in ECE, Chapter 4 on careers in K–12 education, Chapter 5 on educational leadership, Chapter 6 on educational consultants and specialists, Chapter 7 on college and university teaching, Chapter 8 on nonprofit organizations, Chapter 9 on counseling and school psychology, Chapter 10 on applied behavioral analysis, Chapter 11 on child life specialists and other health careers, Chapter 12 on additional careers within the field such as occupational therapy, Chapter 13 on self-reflection, and Chapter 14 on career preparation.

Reflective Questions

1. Why do you want to pursue a career in the field of child and adolescent development?
2. How do you feel about working with culturally and linguistically diverse children and adolescents?
3. What career is most interesting to you in this field of study?
4. What degree(s) do you think you will need for your desired career?

References

Copple, C., & Bredekamp, S. (2009). *Developmentally appropriate practice in early childhood programs serving children from birth through age 8*. Washington, DC: National Association for the Education of Young Children.

Eccles, J. S., Wong, C. A., & Peck, S. C. (2006). Ethnicity as a social context for the development of African-American adolescents. *Journal of School Psychology, 44*(5), 407–426.

Freire, P. (1996). *Pedagogy of the oppressed* (revised). New York: Continuum.

Harven, A. M., & Soodjinda, D. (2016). Pedagogical strategies for challenging students' world views. In *Social Justice Instruction* (pp. 3–14). Basel, Switzerland: Springer International Publishing.

Hewett, V. M. (2001). Examining the Reggio Emilia approach to early childhood education. *Early Childhood Education Journal, 29*(2), 95–100.

Ladson-Billings, G. (1995). But that's just good teaching! The case for culturally relevant pedagogy. *Theory into Practice, 34*(3), 159–165.

Ladson-Billings, G. (2014). Culturally relevant pedagogy 2.0: Aka the remix. *Harvard Educational Review, 84*(1), 74–84.

Lee, S. J. (1994). Behind the model-minority stereotype: Voices of high-and low-achieving Asian American students. *Anthropology & Education Quarterly, 25*(4), 413–429.

Lowe, R. (2009). Childhood through the ages. In *An introduction to early childhood studies* (pp. 21–32). London: Sage Publications.

McAllister, G., & Irvine, J. J. (2000). Cross cultural competency and multicultural teacher education. *Review of Educational Research, 70*(1), 3–24.

Noguera, P. A. (2003a). Schools, prisons, and social implications of punishment: Rethinking disciplinary practices. *Theory into Practice, 42*(4), 341–350.

Noguera, P. A. (2003b). The trouble with Black boys: The role and influence of environmental and cultural factors on the academic performance of African American males. *Urban Education, 38*(4), 431–459.

Reynolds, R. (2010). They think you're lazy, and other messages Black parents send their Black sons: An exploration of critical race theory in the examination of educational outcomes for Black males. *Journal of African American Males in Education, 1*, 144–163.

Rinaldi, C. (1993). The emergent curriculum and social constructivism. In *The hundred languages of children: The Reggio Emilia approach to early childhood education* (pp. 101–111). Greenwich, CT: Ablex Publishing Corporation.

Wong, C. A., Eccles, J. S., & Sameroff, A. (2003). The influence of ethnic discrimination and ethnic identification on African American adolescents' school and socioemotional adjustment. *Journal of Personality, 71*(6), 1197–1232.

Chapter 2

Examining Career Theory
and Metaphors

The first chapter of this textbook introduced you to the field of child and adolescent development. This second chapter briefly introduces you to the field of career theory and practice. The goal is to give you a broad perspective to guide you as a student majoring in child and adolescent development or a related field to find the best possible career fit for you at this time and place among the numerous choices available to you. So, continue to read this chapter to discover the field of career theory and metaphors, and how it applies to you and your future career decisions.

Overview of Career Theory

Inkson (2007) states that career theorists and practitioners have recognized the complexity of careers. There are nine or more career metaphors that may operate during a person's career trajectory at any given time. A career trajectory is unique to each person and creates a story that only applies to that person. According to Inkson (2007), everyone's career story contains several elements, including key characters, success strategies, delicate management, pivotal decisions, gathering of information, and finding a job. The elements may go in any order and can be repeated or skipped because careers are so complex; everyone has a different story.

At this point in the chapter, although it is only the beginning, you may be asking yourself what the definition of "career" is. You may have come to the understanding that a career is more complex than you could have imagined. Here we offer a definition of the concept. The *Merriam-Webster* online dictionary defines "career" as a period of time spent in a job or profession or a job followed as a life's work. The Google dictionary defines career as a noun and a verb. According to Google, career as a noun is "an occupation undertaken for a significant period of a person's life and with opportunities for progress." Career as a verb is "to move swiftly and in an uncontrolled way in a specified direction." The last definition of career to state is from Dictionary.com, which has two definitions, for a noun and a verb, that we are sourcing for this chapter. This source states that a career is "an occupation or profession, especially one requiring special training, followed as one's lifework." The second definition from Dictionary.com is "a person's progress or general course of action through life or through a phase of life, as in some profession or undertaking." There are other definitions on Dictionary.com, but these are the ones used for this chapter.

After reading the various definitions presented in the previous paragraph, you probably conclude that the word "career" is complex and holds different meanings for different people. What does career mean to you? Where are you in your career journey? The best definition for this textbook or for readers who are experiencing this textbook is, perhaps, the second definition from Dictionary.com. Our preferred definition shows that careers are active and not static and can be over an entire lifespan or take place only in one phase of life. Lastly, this definition of career also suggests that career actions and spans can be different for each person.

As you begin looking at the careers in the field of child and adolescent development, what are your thoughts? Where are you now? Are you a college student right out of high school or an older adult returning to college? Where do you see yourself in the future? How much education do you want to get and what degrees do you want to achieve? Do you want to change your career direction without any further education? Perhaps you are mid-career and you want a change? Maybe you are retired from one career, but you want to feel useful in another career field such as child and adolescent development? No matter where you are starting, your options for your career trajectory are numerous and practically limitless.

Careers can be varied, but can also be narrow in some ways. Now, we give the readers an even broader perspective by introducing some of the various career theories that exist in the literature. This information demonstrates just how varied perspectives on careers can be. Most importantly, understanding these various theoretical perspectives may help you on your career journey. As you read about these various theories, you can decide which theoretical perspective fits you and your situation the best.

Some Theoretical Perspectives on Careers

We present the theoretical perspectives in relatively historical order. This is because we believe that it is best to be eclectic and use aspects of all the theories as the career situation dictates. This chapter will present six theories that may help you think about your career choice:

1. career construction theory;
2. social cognitive career theory;
3. John Holland's career theory;
4. systems theory framework of career development;
5. happenstance learning theory; and
6. chaos theory of careers.

We begin our relatively historical walk through career theories with career construction theory. Career construction theory is the work of Super (1953, 1980) and Savickas (2002, 2005). In this theory a person's career develops along with his or her "work self-concept." A work self-concept comprises thoughts and beliefs about the self that pertain to job processes and job environments. In other words, as a person develops his or her work self-concept, he or she tries various jobs and job environments to assess the fit with his or her work self-concept. The more we develop and become self-aware as people, the more we understand and come to know the type of job, career, and work environment that is best for ourselves. In this theory people actively create their careers with intent and purpose.

The next theory to be presented is social cognitive career theory (Lent, Brown, & Hackett, 1994, 2002; Olson, 2014). This theory is grounded in the leading psychological theory of social cognition (Bandura, 1986), which states that an individual's self-knowledge is directly related to the context of social interactions, experiences, and media influences. According to social cognitive career theory, your career is framed by perceptions of your abilities and your beliefs about what will happen when you use the abilities. Social cognitive career theorists take the basics of Bandura's theory and create a model that forecasts a

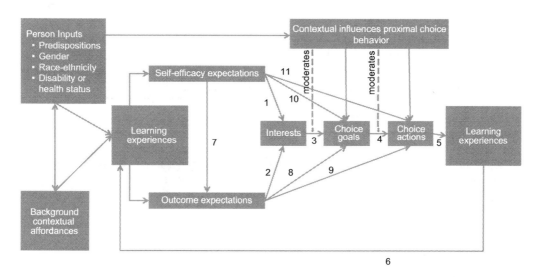

Figure 2.1 Prediction of Vocational Choice in Social Cognitive Career Theory

person's career choice (see Figure 2.1). In this model, personal characteristics and environmental supports and constraints combine with your interests, goals, and actions to create a career choice. For example, you consider your own characteristics to develop your self-efficacy beliefs. You also examine environmental opportunity and constraints to consider what one believes is realistically possible. All of this information plus interests and goals, combine to help you make a career choice.

John Holland (1970, 1973, 1985, 1997) is a career counselor who created his own career theory and assessment instruments. His vocational personality theory is quite influential in the world of career theorists and counselors. Holland matched vocational personality types with work environments and created six pairs: conventional, realistic, investigative, artistic, social, and enterprising. According to this theory, people with conventional characteristics should pursue a conventional career. In other words, your type gives you information about what career you should have. More information about Holland's theory is in Chapter 13 of this textbook.

Systems theories are usually multifaceted and eclectic, considering all aspects of a phenomenon. In other words, systems theories have many pieces that fit together and relate to each other. The systems theory framework of career development (McMahon, 2011) combines factors from various theories of career development into one theoretical framework or model. Some of the main contributions of this framework are the recognition of career development as multifaceted, ever-changing, and flowing, with connecting factors and systems that influence each other. In other words, careers have many pieces—individual, social, and environmental-societal—that influence each other in a bi-directional fashion. Your career is made of individual, social, and environmental-societal pieces in a systematic fashion. The complex interactions among these pieces work to create your career journey, which can be circular, repetitive, and/or unpredictable.

A relatively new career theory is happenstance learning theory, which was developed by Krumboltz (2009). With this theory, Krumboltz (2009) and others (Krumboltz, Foley, & Cotter, 2013) assert that the distinction between career and personal counseling is blurred.

In other words, career and personal counseling are similar in some way. For example, proponents of happenstance learning theory put forth the idea that career counselors must assist their clients with psychological issues like persistence and depression or the emotions that come from discrimination and other discouragements. Krumboltz (2009) states that career counselors must help their clients solve life's problems and lead the life that they find desirable in their career and life beyond careers. Krumboltz (2009) also states that counseling should focus on client behaviors and assessments should enrich client learning. In other words, whether or not career counseling is on the right path is determined by the client's success outside of the session in terms of their career and personal life. The relevance of this career theory is that you may need career counseling or coaching to aid you in finding your career path and journey. Additionally, this theory accompanies the assessment instrument that Krumboltz created that is mentioned in Chapter 13 of this textbook, the Career Beliefs Inventory (Krumboltz, 1994, 2009).

The last career theory to be discussed in this chapter is chaos theory of careers (Pryor & Bright, 2011). There are four main factors in this career theory; complexity, change, chance, and construction. Complexity is the reality that career decisions are interconnected and unpredictable. Change is recognizing that changes from small to large will happen in a career. Chance is accepting that people cannot control or predict all that occurs in their career. Construction is a person's active pursuit and design of his or her career future. The multidimensional nature of chaos theory of careers allows anyone to simultaneously consider many factors of a career decision.

Using a career theory is one method for understanding a person's career trajectories and journeys. Metaphors can also be used to describe and understand careers (Inkson, 2007). Metaphors are figures of speech that capture the essence of some phenomenon. The next section of this chapter defines and describes some of the various metaphors of careers, jobs, and work. Much of this section comes from the ideas and work of Inkson (2007).

Career Metaphors

There are numerous metaphors that can describe careers, jobs, and work. One true career metaphor does not exist, but one or more of the metaphors presented here may ring true for you. Indeed it is not unusual for more than one metaphor to apply to a person's career story and history (Inkson, 2007). As you read about the various career metaphors put forth by Inkson (2007), you may find that elements of more than one of the metaphors are true for you. Nine career metaphors are discussed here: inheritance, cycles, action, fit, journey, roles, relationships, resources, and career stories.

Inheritance. Upon birth people receive inheritances from their parents and other family members and sometimes from friends. For instance, friends can contribute to your socioeconomic status. These inheritances include genes and biology, gender, ethnic group, socioeconomic status, family structure, culture and language, and country of origin. They lay the foundation for a person's skills and ability development, characteristics, values, and educational attainment. Depending on the inheritances that you have, you may have stepping stones (opportunities and access) to a great career or be "imprisoned" (limited by environmental or personal conditions) by negative, dead-end career choices (Inkson, 2007). However, the aim of this textbook is to help all those who major in child and adolescent development to find personally fulfilling and rewarding careers and career stories. Inheritance is one metaphor that often gets little discussion in career textbooks (Inkson, 2007).

Cycles. This career metaphor refers to stages, phases, or seasons of your work life. Although Erik Erikson is a psychologist most often cited in child and adolescent development textbooks, he is also sometimes cited in career theory or career development textbooks. His stage theory of psychosocial development is a wonderful metaphor for work life (Inkson, 2007). In Erikson's theory, he describes stages or phases of life. Inkson's application of Erikson's theory shows us that age is related to career development and his theory adds a bit of predictability to our possible career trajectories, if indeed careers follow along with his theoretical stages.

Super (1957, 1990) and Levinson (1986) discuss stages to career growth and development. Super's theory was discussed previously in this chapter. His ideas are mentioned again here because his ideas fit the cycle metaphor of careers. Super's propositions discuss the construction of careers in stages from growth to disengagement. Levinson's ideas are also included in some textbooks on career theory and career practice. He states that there are three main phases, or seasons, of adult life: early, middle, and late. Each season has subphases. For instance, middle life includes transitions at ages 40, 50, and 60 years. Our careers change in each of these phases.

Action. With the action metaphor, people use their *behaviors, agency,* and *self-expression* to plan and construct their careers. These three terms can be defined and described in different ways. For the purposes of this textbook, behaviors are observable actions that you perform and agency is the belief that you have skills and abilities that will produce positive outcomes. Self-expression is your own unique manner of communicating thoughts, ideas, and characteristics. When making career decisions, you use your behaviors, agency, and self-expression to reason. This thinking and reasoning leads to action that is based on behaviors, agency, and self-expression.

Fit. This career metaphor seems most intuitive. In this textbook, we are trying to help you find a career fit, and by reading this textbook, you are taking some action to find a career fit. In order to find a career fit, you must be knowledgeable of your abilities, skills, and characteristics. You must also know the requirements of certain jobs and work environments. Other personal factors, such as values and interests, can also come into play. Environmental factors such as opportunities and access can also influence career fit. Additionally, to find a career fit, it is wise to take action and not just understand, realize, or assess personal factors. In other words, through internships, apprenticeships, and actual work experience you can truly come to test out the fit of a particular career area. These types of actions also help you to truly understand work requirements and vocational environments as well. Therefore we believe that the metaphor of fit is related to the metaphor of action. Indeed all career metaphors and theories can be interrelated.

Journey. This metaphor is relatable for laypeople in addition to experts in the field. Indeed, "career journey" is a term used frequently in this textbook. Another term used somewhat interchangeably is "career trajectory." When thinking of your career as a journey, you will emphasize factors such as your career's uniqueness, path, and speed. The career journey includes beginnings, turns, plateaus, and destinations. Some of the career journey types are linear, spiral, steady-state, transitory, professional, bureaucratic, and entrepreneurial (Driver, 1979; Kanter, 1989). For linear, you go in a straight line. For spiral, you turn around and advance or get a promotion, much as a spiral staircase. For steady-state, you seem to plateau for a time. For transitory, a certain job is for a specific period of time. Professional, bureaucratic, and entrepreneurial refer to the type of job: for example, professional could refer to legal, academic, or medical careers; bureaucratic career journeys concern jobs with a government or other agency; the entrepreneurial type refers to being your own boss.

Roles. Your role is the function that you play in a setting or process. You have a number of roles in various settings such as family and community, including the role you play in your career. Indeed, you may have many roles (functions) in your career at the same time period or at different time periods. Usually, a single job or career involves more than one role. For instance, the job of professor has three main roles: teaching, conducting research, and providing service. In addition, society assigns roles to certain jobs and careers. For examples, teachers often have a parental role and health practitioners have a helping role. In other words, your role in society depends on your job or career. A counselor plays a different role than a family lawyer, preschool teacher, child life specialist, or a children's minister. These are all jobs related to the field of child and adolescent development. Various roles are given to these jobs by society. Throughout your career, you must balance all of the roles and solve the occasional conflict among the numerous roles that you play. Sometimes, the career role or roles can become a huge part of how you identify yourself. Sometimes, the career role is a larger part of your identity than family or community or any other role. At other times or for other people, the career role may take a back seat to family and community roles. Ideally, a person has balance between all roles concerning career, family, and community.

Relationships. This interesting metaphor examines a person's level of career connectedness and individualism. All careers contain a certain amount of both connectedness and individualism. The exact percentages or levels vary with different careers and in different time periods or career tasks. In general, it is good to connect through activities such as networking, improving your social capital, and finding mentors. Networking is placing yourself in social situations where you can make contacts with people who can aid you on your career journey. Social capital is the amount of influence and resources you have in your social networks of people and institutions and organizations. A mentor is someone who gives emotional and social support, as well as sage career advice and information. A wise career strategy includes all three: networking, improving social capital, and finding mentors. Another element of the relationship metaphor is your own unique personal influence and individualism. This is perhaps the most important element of your career relationships. How much power and positive energy do you generate in your career networks? What percentage of your career actions are focused on you and what percentage on other people in the environment? Personal influence may be one of the biggest impacts on your career trajectory.

Resources. This metaphor acknowledges that control of a person's career is not totally his or her own. The institutions and organizations that employ people have an influence over their careers. Institutions and organizations have priorities, practices, and resource needs that determine how people's careers will progress. However, some institutions and organizations see their employees as valuable resources and they offer training and some joint decision-making for employees. Additionally, employers assess the value of employee's resources on a regular basis. Employees typically receive an evaluation about how effective they have been for their employers. Therefore, when making career decisions think about how a potential employing organization views its employees. It is also wise to realize that your employer possesses some control over your career decisions and paths.

Career stories. We all have stories to tell about how we obtained our job, what we do, and the meaning our jobs have for us. Our career stories contain our personal beliefs about our careers, including how we identify, what our career means, and our future goals and plans. These stories vary in their relationship to reality and not everyone will see a career story in the same manner.

These career metaphors and the previous career theories are frameworks for examining your career. They can also be utilized to make career decisions and choices. One of the biggest career choices or decisions you can make is what career is the right one for you. To do this you will want to examine your skills, abilities, characteristics, values, and interests. You will also want some information about the settings and environments and preparations necessary for various careers. Then you will need some experiences with some careers. The proper educational preparation, such as a BA in child and adolescent development, is a must. Then you may need to continue on from there with additional degrees (for example, an MS in nursing, PhD in counseling, JD in family law, or other degrees). You may also need some sort of certification (Behavior Analyst or others) or a credential (teaching credential or administrative services credential) or some other classes. You may also need to take extra tests (a state bar exam, for example). This is the purpose of this textbook is helping those who major in child and adolescent development or a related field on their career journeys.

At this point, we suggest that you take some time to reflect on the information you have absorbed thus far in the textbook. Then think about yourself and some possible career options. What educational preparation is necessary for that position or those positions? Will there be other requirements such as permits, licenses, credentials, or internships? Just ponder those questions and then read on about some specifics of preparing for the world of work and some specifics of various careers.

Summary

In this chapter you have received some information about career theories and career metaphors and practical career strategies. You discovered that current career theorists and practitioners use the theory that best fits the situation and their client. You also learned about how career metaphors can be helpful in understanding and charting a career path. This information could have been presented in a more elaborate way. However, these brief introductions were meant to give you a broad understanding of some career theory concepts. This information combined with child and adolescent development theoretical information can help you to choose your own career path and trajectory.

Reflective Questions

1. How much did you know about career theories and metaphors before reading this chapter?
2. Which theory and metaphor do you think best fit your current situation?
3. Which metaphor best fits your current situation?
4. What insights have you gained about yourself?
5. What insights have you gained about the world of work and careers?

References

Bandura, A. (1986). *Social foundations of thought and action: A social cognitive theory*. Englewood Cliffs, NJ: Prentice Hall.

Driver, M. J. (1979). Career concepts and career management in organizations. In C. L. Cooper (Ed.), *Behavioral problems in organizations* (pp. 79–139). Englewood Cliffs, NJ: Prentice Hall.

Holland, J. L. (1970). *The self directed search*. Odessa, FL: Psychological Assessment Resources, Inc.

Holland, J. L. (1973). *Making vocational choices*. Englewood Cliffs, NJ: Prentice Hall.

Holland, J. L. (1985). *Making vocational choices* (2nd ed.). Englewood Cliffs, NJ: Prentice Hall.

Holland, J. L. (1997). *Making vocational choices: A theory of vocational personalities and work environments* (2nd ed.). Odessa, FL: Psychological Assessment Resources.

Inkson, K. (2007). *Understanding careers: The metaphors of working lives*. Thousand Oaks, CA: Sage Publications.

Kanter, R. M. (1989). Careers and the wealth of nations: A macro-perspective on the structure and implications of career forms. In M. B. Arthur, D. T. Hall, & B. S. Lawrence (Eds.), *Handbook of career theory* (pp. 506–521). Cambridge, UK: Cambridge University Press.

Krumboltz, J. D. (1994). The career beliefs inventory. *Journal of Counseling & Development, 72,* 424–428.

Krumboltz, J. D. (2009). The happenstance learning theory. *Journal of Career Assessment, 17,* 135–154.

Krumboltz, J. D., Foley, P. F., & Cotter, E. W. (2013). Applying the happenstance learning theory to involuntary career transitions. *The Career Development Quarterly, 61,* 15–26.

Lent, R. W., Brown, S. D., & Hackett, G. (1994). Towards a unifying social cognitive theory of career and academic interest, choice, and performance. *Journal of Vocational Behavior, 45,* 79–122.

Lent, R. W., Brown, S. D., & Hackett, G. (2002). Social cognitive career theory. In D. Brown & Associates (Eds.), *Career choice and development* (4th ed., pp. 255–311). San Francisco: Jossey-Bass.

Levinson, D. J. (1986). A conception of adult development. *American Psychologist, 46,* 3–13.

McMahon, M. (2011). The systems theory framework of career development. *Journal of Employment Counseling, 48,* 170–172.

Olson, J. S. (2014). Opportunities, obstacles, and options: First generation college graduates and social cognitive career theory. *Journal of Career Development, 41*(3), 199–217.

Pryor, R., & Bright, J. (2011). *The chaos theory of careers*. New York, NY: Routledge.

Savickas, M. L. (2002). Career construction: A developmental theory of career behavior. In D. Brown & Associates (Eds.), *Career choice and development* (4th ed., pp. 149–205). San Francisco: Jossey-Bass.

Savickas, M. L. (2005). The theory and practice of career construction. In S. D. Brown & R. W. Lent (Eds.), *Career development and counseling: Putting theory and research to work* (pp. 42–70). Hoboken, NJ: Wiley.

Super, D. E. (1953). A theory of vocational development. *American Psychologist, 30,* 88–92.

Super, D. E. (1957). *The psychology of careers*. New York: Harper & Row.

Super, D. E. (1980). A life-span, life-space approach to career development. *Journal of Vocational Behavior, 16,* 282–298.

Super, D. E. (1990). A life-span, life-space approach to career development. In D. Brown, L. Brooks, & Associates (Eds.), *Career choice and development* (2nd ed., pp. 197–261). San Francisco: Jossey-Bass.

Part 2

Careers

Chapter 3

Careers in ECE
(Birth to Third Grade)

Part 1 of this textbook helped you to get started thinking about careers in child and adolescent development. In Chapter 1, you were introduced to the field of child and adolescent development. Additionally, you get a glimpse of career theories and metaphors. Part 2, the bulk of the textbook, introduces you to various careers that are possible with a degree in child and adolescent development. You will be introduced in depth to more than nine career fields and you will also be given brief introductions to more than a dozen other possibilities. As you will come to see, a degree in child and adolescent development is a great foundation for a whole host of careers that involve children and families. We begin this exploration of careers by examining career paths in ECE.

ECE is a traditional career within the field of child and adolescent development. It is one of the career areas that is often associated with a degree in child and adolescent development. This field of education includes teaching infants to third graders. However, this is not the only career you can have with a degree in child and adolescent development. This book describes a number of careers in the field of child and adolescent development. Additionally, the actual jobs within ECE are probably more varied and diverse than you currently imagine. You can do more in ECE than teach children, because the field is developing and changing. There is and has been an emphasis on changing policies and improving quality, in addition to inviting and retaining more men in the field (Cooney & Bittner, 2001). So let us begin exploring ECE careers.

Child and Adolescent Development as a Foundation

If you are familiar with ECE, you know that you can enter the field as an assistant teacher with a high school diploma or general equivalency degree (GED). Then you can move up the ladder to associate teacher with nine or so postsecondary units and be a lead teacher with approximately 24 to 30 units of college-level ECE units. The policies surrounding this particular career ladder are changing. Indeed, in some states and in some positions the new policies are in place already (Brizzi, 1997; Burbank & Wiefek, 2001; Professional Preparation and Development Committee of the Vermont Early Childhood Work Group, 1998). The new policies aim at improving quality and requiring a full BA degree for many positions in ECE, such as lead teacher, parent educator, afterschool director, curriculum specialist, early interventionist, and family child care operator. In some cases, a child and adolescent development degree is needed. Sometimes, however, an equivalent degree such as psychology, sociology, or education is acceptable for these positions. We believe that a degree in child and adolescent development is better preparation for the field of ECE, because of the invaluable knowledge and skills obtained. What are the unique knowledge and skills obtained?

With a degree in child and adolescent development you learn the milestones and phases children have as they are growing. You also get a strong theoretical understanding of the appropriate processes and strategies to use to teach children. You get a glimpse at how the early years impact the later years, too. You view the child as a whole human being with more than just cognitive and intellectual development. You see how the various areas of development impact each other, such as how emotional and social development and language development impact cognition and intellectual skills and abilities. With a degree in child and adolescent development, you also get a sense of how families and communities impact children and impact children's growth and development. In sum, a degree in child and adolescent development is targeted at understanding children and also allows for a broader view of influences than just cognition. For instance, biology, physical development, families, communities, and the general environment can also influence children. To learn this and understand this, studying child and adolescent development is a plus.

Possible Jobs in ECE

As mentioned earlier in this chapter, there are other positions besides teacher in the field of ECE. In addition, there are typically levels related to teacher positions. For instance, three levels of teacher positions are assistant teacher, associate teacher, and lead teacher (see Table 3.1). Moreover, teachers can work with either infants, toddlers, or preschoolers. Some of the other positions include afterschool teacher, afterschool director, family child care operator, early intervention specialist, parent educator, home-based teacher, curriculum specialist, health specialist, and parent liaison (see Table 3.2). The job of a preschool /child care center director or manager will also be discussed in this chapter.

Transitional kindergarten teacher is a relatively new position. This position is different than a preschool teacher, because the focus is more stringently school readiness and the position more often requires a teaching credential in addition to a BA degree. Transitional kindergarten teachers are almost always hired by an elementary school and are usually governed by different policies than a teacher in a preschool center. This happens even though some of the children are the same age in both of the diverse settings.

So, what do you do in these jobs?

Table 3.1 Levels of ECE Teachers

Level	Description
Assistant Teacher	You can start with minimal education such as a high school diploma or GED, and you will need much supervision and professional development on the job.
Associate Teacher	You can start with some relevant ECE units in college (ranges from 12 to 30 or so units), but you also need a year or two of experience. You will need some supervision and professional development while on the job.
Lead Teacher	You need an AA for some programs and BA or MA for others. You usually need three or more years of experience, can work with some autonomy, and can supervise others. You still have to report to a director or manager and will receive additional professional development on the job.

Table 3.2 Other ECE Positions

Position	Description
Afterschool teacher	Supervise and teach children before and after school.
Afterschool Director	Coordinate and manage afterschool programs.
Family Child Care Operator	Operate early child care as a business in your own home.
Early Intervention Specialist	Work with young children who have special needs.
Parent Educator	Give parenting workshops to parents with young children.
Home-based Teacher	Go into children's homes. Interact with and teach both the children and their parents.
Curriculum Specialist	Create or adapt and manage curriculum.
Health Specialist	Teach children, parents, and staff about good health practices.
Parent Liaison	Serve as a communication link between ECE programs and parents or other family members.

Let us begin with the job of the teacher. In general, the job of a teacher contains more than just teaching. Some of those additional duties are planning, writing lesson plans, observing children formally and informally, assessing children formally and informally, communicating with parents, completing paperwork, cooking meals and snacks, as well as helping younger students with health, hygiene, self-help skills, and general caretaking. Teachers also have to attend staff meetings and complete professional development/ training on a regular basis. These duties are associated with teaching all age groups of children to varying levels. (See Figures 3.1 and 3.2 for typical daily schedules in early elementary settings.)

Additionally, the job of a teacher varies with the setting. For instance, a teacher will have completely different duties depending on whether he or she teaches in a public state, public university, public federal, private locally owned, private national-chain franchise, or private faith-based setting. As an example, in faith-based settings you are required to hold a certain set of beliefs, to teach the beliefs, and to pray to some deity. Public federal settings, for example, usually require a lot more paperwork than any other setting. This is because of the standards and regulations that must be met and evaluated. In some settings, teachers write their own lessons and curriculum. In other settings, such national-chain franchises, a curriculum may be provided or nonexistent. In general though, the job of a teacher is to educate children broadly and care for them.

Some teachers in the field of ECE teach young elementary school children in first through third grades. The National Association of the Education of Young Children (NAEYC) considers those grades to be in the ECE field. The NAEYC has written standards and guidelines for those grade levels. Some of these standards, such as ethics, are discussed in this chapter. Majoring in child and adolescent development can also prepare you for a career of teaching in the early elementary grades. A credential is usually needed in addition to the degree. However, it should be noted that a degree in child and adolescent development is a good foundation for teaching in the early elementary grades. Indeed, some states, such as California, allows child and adolescent development majors with a credential to also teach upper elementary grades and middle school.

7:30	Arrive at school and set up for the day.
8:15	Yard duty before school.
9:00	Math.
10:00	Reading.
10:45	Recess—Yard duty.
11:00	PE.
11:30	Social studies.
12:15	Lunch.
12:35	Recess—Yard duty.
1:00	Spelling.
1:30	Project-based learning.
2:15	Science.
3:00	Clean up/homework.
3:20	Dismissal—Yard duty.
4:00	Correct work and prepare for tomorrow.
5:30	Head home.

Figure 3.1 Public School Second Grade Schedule

7:45	Arrive at school and set up for the day.
8:20	Opening routine.
9:00	Math.
9:50	Snack.
10:00	Recess.
10:15	PE.
10:45	Language arts.
11:30	French/Spanish.
12:00	Lunch.
12:20	Recess.
12:40	Class time.
2:00	Music.
2:40	Closing routine.
2:55	Dismissal.

Figure 3.2 Private School Second Grade Schedule

What about being a director of an ECE center? What does that person do and what are the qualifications for that role? Let us begin by discussing qualifications. Directors usually have a postsecondary degree, meaning at least a BA and in some cases a MA or doctorate. Directors usually have some experience as an early childhood teacher and have perhaps been a mentoring teacher or curriculum specialist. Other qualifications that vary by state and regional areas include special permits or credentials or coursework in educational administration. Employment in the position of director is possible with these qualifications.

The everyday life of a director can be unpredictable. They can greet parents in the morning, solve problems, observe teachers and other employees, hire employees, and evaluate employees. They have to support teachers and other employees, as well as provide professional development opportunities for the teachers. Sometimes directors even purchase groceries and educational supplies needed for the center, or they even teach children for periods of time. Directors lead teachers, so they need to have a vision for the future and be able to manage a budget. In some ways, the director performs much as a principal does, with a difference in the age of the children and the numbers of children and staff involved.

Just reading the previous paragraphs may be educational to you. The job of ECE teachers and directors may be more comprehensive than you first realized. What about the other early childhood positions? What duties are associated with those jobs? For instance, what does an afterschool teacher do and what does an afterschool director do?

Afterschool teachers usually watch over children when the academic school day ends in elementary and middle school settings until the children are retrieved by their parents. This includes helping with homework and monitoring their play. Sometimes, there are official afterschool programs that focus on supplementing the academic day. These programs may focus on science, technology, engineering, and mathematics (STEM); on the visual and performing arts; or on other academic areas. The afterschool director is in charge of managing the teachers as well as planning and administrating the afterschool program and curriculum.

These positions may not be of interest to you, because you want to work with parents of young children. In that case, you can be a parent educator or home-based teacher. Parent educators can work in conjunction with school districts, hospitals, or federal Head Start/Early Head Start programs. In general, you teach child and adolescent theory and research as well as parenting skills and guidance processes to the parents of young children. If you want to be a parent educator in a hospital setting, you may be required to have a background in nursing in addition to child and adolescent development. As a home-based educator, you also can work in the same settings mentioned earlier (public, private, faith based) with a similar background in terms of education and training. The differences are that you go into the home to work with parents and their children. You still focus on educating and training the parents, but you go to their homes and their children are directly involved, too.

A national credential does exist for working in the field of ECE, the Child Development Associate (CDA) and it has been adopted by 46 states (Counsel for Professional Regulation, 2010). This credential is not always a requirement, but it can help a person begin in the field. To obtain a CDA, a person can take courses in Introductory Early Childhood Education and Child and Adolescent Development. Afterwards, two courses that relate specifically to the CDA are taken. The credential is obtained by contacting the Counsel for Professional Regulation directly, as they are responsible for regulating, assessing, and conferring the CDA.

Early Head Start and Head Start: Federal ECE Positions

Early Head Start and Head Start are federal programs that offer ECE positions. The general Head Start programs were started in 1965 and continue through today, while Early Head Start programs began in 1995 (Office of Head Start 2014a, 2014b, 2015a, and 2015b). Head Start serves 4- and 5-year-old children and their families and Early Head Start serves infant and toddlers under the age of 3 and their families. To date, these programs have served more than 32 million children. These programs have changed over the years as a result of evaluations and assessments of effectiveness. In 2007, the programs were reauthorized with support from both Democrats and Republicans. Currently, a BA degree in child and adolescent development or a related field is preferred to be a teacher in Head Start (ACF, 2015).

Since these programs are comprehensive, they offer several services besides education. For example, Head Start offers nutrition and health programs, including dental and mental health. It offers parent support and education/training workshops. There are also special programs for Native Americans and migrant farm worker communities. This program also strives to be culturally responsive, as the population of children and families served is diverse (see Figure 3.3).

Head Start and Early Head Start offer a variety of positions besides teacher and assistant teacher. Nurses and nurses' aides may work in these programs. Of course, there are directors and managers of various levels. Additionally, there are data managers, parent liaisons, health coordinators, and education coordinators. Each program is configured a bit differently depending on the state and agency in which it is housed. These ECE positions are

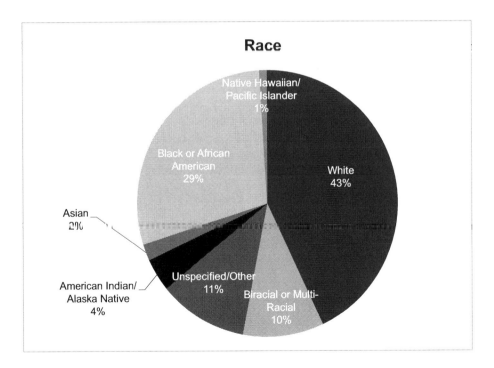

Figure 3.3 Population Served

Source: Head Start Program Facts Fiscal Year 2015

often coveted in the field, because of the tie with the federal government. However, there is also much paperwork to complete in order to document compliance with federal regulations.

Career Paths in ECE

As you will learn in Chapter 13, careers can take many different paths. In the field of ECE, careers can start with a high school diploma or GED and the beginning title is usually one of assistant teacher. These careers usually progress as high as master teacher, director, or curriculum specialist. For advanced positions, a Masters or sometimes a Doctoral degree are usually necessary along with requisite experience. For instance, the state of Washington proposed a career ladder (Burbank & Wiefek, 2001) that describes how you can move up the pay scale with the following education and credentials:

- The basic is the CDA credential for the assistant teacher.
- Next is ECE certification through the state system.
- This is followed by regular academic degrees (AA, BA, and MA) in child and adolescent development or a related field.

Additionally your pay increases with each year of service and increases in responsibilities. The situation in Vermont is very similar, with some variation. The lowest level of a position as exemplified in Vermont is a para-educator, who may be a parent of a child in the program. This is followed by a teacher assistant, a teacher, a specialized teacher, and then a teacher/assistant director. Sometimes, in Vermont, teachers with extensive experience become full directors, parent educators, resource and referral specialists, or home visitors, or assume other positions in ECE.

Let us take an in-depth look at three real-life career paths with a set of interviews. Two of the interviewees work with young children and one interviewee teaches second grade. Right away you will notice the variation in career paths. (The names used in this chapter are pseudonyms.) One path is represented by Alice, who is currently the director at a private, nonprofit, faith-based preschool. Alice began her path as a Pre-K teacher in an elementary school setting. The second career path is represented by Jean. She began her career path in a private elementary school and currently is the director of a public nonprofit infant/toddler program that is connected to a university. In her current position, she also has parent educator responsibilities. The third path is traveled by Annette. She is a second grade teacher in a private, independent school. She began her career by substitute teaching. It is important to note that the degrees obtained in these real-life scenarios are related to child and adolescent development, but are not actually and directly in child and adolescent development. However, an Associate's degree or Bachelor's degree in child and adolescent development will prepare you just as well or better for a career in ECE.

Alice's Interview

Alice lives in Florida and has been in the field of ECE for more than 14 years. She has a Bachelor's degree in elementary education and two credentials from the state of Florida. One credential is for an ECE staff position and the other is for an ECE director position.

Alice has a brother four years older than she is, but when she was 8 years old and her parents divorced she became the only child in the household with her mother. Her mother remarried when Alice was 12 years of age; about that time she began babysitting. When

Alice entered college she did not intend to major in elementary education; however, she declared this major in her sophomore year. She really enjoyed the practicum, internships, and student teaching experiences that were part of her degree; these hands-on experiences were very educational and enjoyable to her.

Currently, Alice is married with three children. When her oldest was 2 years old and her husband finished his formal schooling, she quit teaching in elementary school to be home with her child. At that time, however, a friend asked her to work two days a week in a preschool and invited her to bring her current child and any additional children to work with her. At this juncture in her career, Alice decided to enter ECE and has never looked back. She really enjoys giving children a fun, safe place to learn and grow.

Alice works in a faith-based preschool setting. Even though she came to ECE from a personal need, she feels this is where she should be. In this setting, she has taught children 2 years of age, 4 years of age, 8 years of age, and has been the center director for more than 11 years. She loves her job, especially communicating with and advocating for the children and their families. She has also learned over the years that teaching and educating parents is just as important as caring for and teaching their children.

Although she is the director, she loves getting a chance to go back into the classroom. She loves getting on the floor and entering the children's world. She loves watching timid children grow socially and get excited about school. She feels that her strengths are gaining the trust of parents and communicating that their child is valuable. She thinks that it helps to remember everyone's names, all children and all parents. She greets every child and their parent(s) by name every day.

Jean's Interview

Jean has a BA in elementary education and an MA in ECE that she obtained in Illinois. Both of her parents are only children. Her grandfather on her father's side of the family was a teacher in his early career. Jean is not sure if her family background impacted her decision or not, but seventh grade is the year her quest for becoming an early childhood teacher begins. She babysat and helped with vacation bible school at her church. Jean has children of her own and enjoys having a schedule that is conducive to parenting.

In 1990, she began working in the field at a private elementary school right after obtaining her BA degree (the MA came later). After eight years, she started teaching Pre-K in the setting where she currently works, a public nonprofit infant/toddler program connected to a university. She taught for six years and then was a parent educator in the same setting for three more years. Then she moved to South Carolina, because of her husband's job, where she taught kindergarten in a private school. While in South Carolina, Jean began training early childhood teachers. Four years later, again because of her husband's job, the family moved back to Illinois. She returned to her previous public, nonprofit setting and took the position she currently holds. Jean has enjoyed her career journey and all of the changes and positions.

She says that some of the key points and highlights of her career trajectory are when she finished her MA, when she worked as a parent educator, and when she began training teachers. Obtaining her MA degree helped her to see the importance of the early years in terms of brain development. Becoming a parent educator helped her to see that not every family is the same and that all parents have their own style of parenting. The time that she spent in South Carolina training early childhood teachers gave her a broader perspective of the field, as she learned more about guidelines and requirements.

Jean really enjoys her current position as a center director and parent educator, as it draws on many of her skills and experiences and much of her knowledge base. She basically has three positions: head teacher, parent educator, and director. She also had a chance to write her own job description, as the infant/toddler program was beginning when she was hired. What a nice perk! However, the main reason she loves her job is the joy she finds working with children. She loves watching the infants and toddlers grow as well as interacting and relating with the young children's families.

Lastly, when asked what she brings to the job to make it successful, Jean said she is very caring and loves children. She also mentioned the fact that she demonstrates her knowledge on the job. In other words, she can translate child and adolescent development theory into practice. She said she also brings her love of the job and enthusiasm for it, as well as her commitment for it. Additionally, she says she creates positive experiences, builds good rapport, and engenders mutual respect.

Annette's Interview

Annette is a second grade teacher in a private, independent school that has students from preschool to 12th grade. She has a BA degree in psychology with an emphasis in child psychology that she obtained in New York. She realized after completing college that teaching is what she wanted to do for her life's career. After moving to California, she worked as a substitute teacher and earned a teaching credential. She has been teaching second grade for four years, including her time spent as a substitute teacher.

Annette comes from a family of teachers. Her mother taught science and her father taught high school chemistry after retiring from his career as geologist. Her aunts were teachers and two of her great-grandparents were teachers. She admits that even before she became a teacher she was doing "teaching" all her life with friends and family. Annette does not have her own children yet and she is happy about that situation, because she can focus all her energy on her students.

Some of the key points and highlights of Annette's career journey occurred right after graduating college and during her own childhood. In her early years she was surrounded by teachers and her family taught her to appreciate and respect teachers. She also experienced some wonderful teachers in elementary school. She believes all of this influenced her without her really knowing it. After graduating college she got a job teaching gymnastics and began applying for graduate school in developmental psychology. During this time she realized that graduate school was not her passion, but she really enjoyed being around children and working with them every day. One day she realized that she wanted to teach children and get her credential and that is just what she did. She became a substitute teacher and earned her credential while working in public schools.

As a second grade teacher, her day is scheduled quite strictly. The schedules in the beginning of this chapter are from Annette: one from her public school teaching days and a current one from a private school (see Figures 3.1 and 3.2). Annette has enjoyed both of her schedules, but finds that teaching at a private school gives her more autonomy and freedom to make decisions.

Annette really loves her job, even the challenges—which she sees as opportunities to learn. She is never bored. She is constantly growing and changing, and so is her job. She is always creating and sometimes makes mistakes. If she makes a mistake she just makes changes and tries again. Some of her biggest joys come from celebrating all kinds of holidays, making up songs as teaching materials, and doing research (for example, to find out if penguins have knees). She also finds that she really misses her students when she is on break. Moreover, even her bad days at work are not bad enough to make her want to quit. Even though her way to teaching was not traditional, she cannot imagine doing anything else with her life.

The characteristics that help her with her job are rolling with the punches and being creative. She says with her job she can and does make plans, but that those plans sometimes have to change. She also says that teachers have to create lesson plans, activities, and curriculum modules. She never knew how much creativity was required to be a teacher and how much creativity she had. She states that these characteristics help her to be a great teacher and that teaching is the most rewarding profession there is.

Career Specifics

Salary

The preceding interviews illustrate variances in career trajectories in ECE. They also demonstrate the love that ECE professionals have for their jobs. In general, ECE professionals are warm-hearted and love the children and families with whom they work. This love sustains them in their career, especially since the pay is not high compared to other professions. Pay in ECE has been a challenge since the beginning, because some see jobs in the ECE field as "glorified babysitting." However, the importance of the field is being elevated with the advent of brain research, an emphasis on early school readiness, and an emphasis on educational standards (NAEYC, 2015).

According to the Bureau of Labor Statistics, a preschool teacher can make anywhere from $13.33 to $15.69 per hour and/or $27,720 to $32,510 yearly (Bureau of Labor Statistics, 2014). If the preschool teaching position is attached to an elementary school and the teacher has a credential, the pay increases. These positions, called "transitional kindergarten teachers" in some states, average around $21.90 an hour and $45,550 a year (Bureau of Labor Statistics, 2014). (See Tables 3.3 and 3.4 for hourly wages and annual mean salaries.) The state of New York pays the highest average wage to regular preschool teachers who are not attached to a school district, which is $20.28 an hour or $42,190 a year (Bureau of Labor Statistics, 2014; see Table 3.5). Having a credential, permit, or certificate to teach in special education can also increase pay.

Table 3.3 Industries With the Highest Level of Employment in This Occupation

Industry	Employment	Percent of Industry Employment	Hourly Mean Wage	Annual Mean Wage
Child Day Care Services	231,990	28.52	$13.33	$27,720
Elementary and Secondary Schools	71,020	0.85	$21.90	$45,550
Individual and Family Services	12,750	0.86	$15.59	$32,420
Religious Organizations	7,950	4.22	$15.45	$32,140
Civic and Social Organizations	7,430	1.93	$15.15	$31,510

Source: Bureau of Labor Statistics—Occupational Employment Statistics, May 2014

Table 3.4 Industries With the Highest Concentration of Employment in This Occupation

Industry	Employment	Percent of Industry Employment	Hourly Mean Wage	Annual Mean Wage
Child Day Care Services	231,990	28.52	$13.33	$27,720
Religious Organizations	7,950	4.22	$15.45	$32,140
Civic and Social Organizations	7,430	1.93	$15.15	$31,510
Social Advocacy Organizations	2,320	1.15	$15.63	$32,510
Individual and Family Services	12,750	0.86	$15.59	$32,420

Source: Bureau of Labor Statistics—Occupational Employment Statistics, May 2014

Table 3.5 States With the Highest Employment Level in This Occupation

State	Employment	Employment per Thousand Jobs	Location Quotient	Hourly Mean Wage	Annual Mean Wage
California	47,030	3.11	1.19	$16.38	$34,070
New York	31,210	3.54	1.36	$20.28	$42,190
Florida	20,660	2.70	1.03	$12.59	$26,180
Illinois	18,680	3.24	1.24	$14.67	$30,510
Texas	18,190	1.62	0.62	$16.99	$35,350

Source: Bureau of Labor Statistics—Occupational Employment Statistics, May 2014

Ethics

The NAEYC has created a set of ethical principles to guide the ECE field (NAEYC, 2005). All professionals in the field should commit to these principles. Since the field of ECE is large and complex, and the positions are wide and varied, numerous principles have been created for professionals to follow. The NAEYC document lists responsibilities to children, families, colleagues, the community and society (NAEYC, 2005). All NAEYC ethical principles are guided by the following core values:

- Appreciate childhood as a unique and valuable stage of the human life cycle.
- Base your work on knowledge of how children develop and learn.
- Appreciate and support the bond between the child and family.
- Recognize that children are best understood and supported in the context of family, culture, community, and society.
- Respect the dignity, worth, and uniqueness of each individual (child, family member, and colleague).
- Respect diversity in children, families, and colleagues.
- Recognize that children and adults achieve their full potential in the context of relationships that are based on trust and respect.

Summary

This chapter described ECE careers, the first set of careers described in this textbook. Careers in ECE are very traditional in the field of child and adolescent development. The most common career is that of the ECE teacher, but there exist other careers in ECE, such as parent educator, family child care provider, and afterschool teacher. Careers in ECE have more depth and variety than most realize. Therefore, starting with a foundation in child and adolescent development is a great beginning to a career in the ECE field.

You may begin in the field of ECE as a para-educator or assistant teacher with a high school diploma. You can also get a CDA credential to begin a career in ECE. However, the field is changing and a BA is now becoming the entry-level degree for many positions. This is especially true for federal positions in programs such as Early Head Start and Head Start. Requirements for and pay in the different positions in ECE vary by state, region, and setting. Your career path can also vary depending on one's ability, educational level, characteristics, years in the field, and the setting in which you work.

Many in the ECE field are drawn to it because of a love for children. They also enjoy seeing lives change, grow, and develop. Nonetheless, some ECE professionals remain in the ECE field for their entire career, especially those with a good foundation in child and adolescent development.

Reflective Questions

1. What are some avenues for communicating to the general public that ECE is more than just "glorified babysitting?"
2. What are your thoughts about transitional kindergarten requiring a credential, even though the children are usually 3 to 5 years old? What are some of the positives that will result from this and what are some concerns?
3. In which ECE program or setting do see yourself fitting the best (federal, state, private, public, infant/toddler, preschool, early elementary?)

Is This Right for You?

When considering the appropriateness of this field for you, your personal characteristics and motives are quite important—and so is considering the low pay. People in the field of ECE are typically very nurturing and patient, with high energy. Of course, they also have a very genuine love for children. They usually start off their career with high expectations, high hopes, and tremendous motivation. However, the low pay and burnout are concerns. Some ECE professionals choose to stay in the field, while others leave.

Nevertheless, right now is an exciting time in the field of ECE. Brain development research findings, the advent of higher degree requirements, and more respect for the ECE field all add up to an exciting and promising time in this career field. With proper preparation educationally and practical experience, you can be well prepared. However, your personal characteristics and motives are quite important in this field, too. Additionally, with research and networking, your career can take you to a place where you are happy and satisfied with your career choice. Taking one day at a time and always putting your best foot forward can help you succeed in the ECE field. Starting with a foundation of child and adolescent development can help you launch a fulfilling career trajectory in the field of ECE.

References

Brizzi, E. (1997). *Developing a Partnership (DAP) in Early Childhood Education: A parent career and employment program.* Los Angles, CA: Los Angles County Office of Education.

Burbank, J. R., & Wiefek, N. (2001). *The Washington State Early Childhood Education Career Development Ladder.* Seattle, WA: Economic Opportunity Inst.

Bureau of Labor Statistics (2014). *Occupational employment and wages.* Retrieved from www.bls. gov/opub/ted/2015/occupational-employment-wages-2014.htm

Cooney, M. H., & Bittner, M. T. (2001). *Men in Early Childhood Education: Their emergent issues.* New York, NY: Human Sciences Press, Inc.

Council for Professional Recognition. (2010). *Child development associate assessment system and competency standards.* Retrieved from http://cdacouncil.org.

Office of Head Start (2014a). *Office of Head Start—Early Head Start Services Snapshot.* Retrieved from http://eclkc.ohs.acf.hhs.gov/hslc/data/psr/2014/NATIONAL_SNAPSHOT_EHS.pdf

Office of Head Start (2014b). *Office of Head Start—Head Start Services Snapshot.* Retrieved from http://eclkc.ohs.acf.hhs.gov/hslc/data/psr/2014/NATIONAL_SNAPSHOT_ALL_PROGRAMS. pdf

Office of Head Start (2015a). *Head Start Program Facts Fiscal year 2015.* Retrieved from https:// eclkc.ohs.acf.hhs.gov/hslc/data/factsheets/docs/head-start-fact-sheet-fy-2015.pdf

Office of Head Start (2015b). *Office of Head Start—History of Head Start.* Retrieved from www. acf.hhs.gov/ohs/about/history-of-head-start

Professional Preparation and Development Committee of the Vermont Early Childhood Work Group (1998). *The Vermont guide to early childhood careers.* Retrieved from http://files.eric. ed.gov/fulltext/ED424979.pdf

Chapter 4

Careers in Middle Elementary Through Adult Education

In the previous chapter, we considered child and adolescent development as a foundation for careers in ECE. This chapter continues the discussion of careers in education by considering careers as an educator working with students in school settings beyond third grade. This will include elementary schools, middle schools, secondary schools, and adult education settings. Becoming a professional educator for youth and adults includes a variety of career options, including public schoolteacher, private schoolteacher, special education professional, and adult education teacher. After defining levels of education, we will look at concepts important to those preparing for a successful career in education. We finally take up the qualifications and requirements necessary to enter the teaching profession, including a discussion of the role of specific state requirements that determine what is required to become a professional educator.

Generally, middle elementary grades are considered to be fourth through sixth grades, although in some school districts, elementary school concludes at sixth grade. The next level of education, secondary school, begins with what is variously known as middle school or junior high school. Typically, middle school encompasses sixth through eighth grades, while junior high school often encompasses seventh through ninth grades. However, in some schools or school districts, junior high school is specified as two years (seventh and eight grades). Each school district independently determines whether it will offer middle school or junior high school; that decision therefore also dictates the configuration of its high schools, often considered the heart of secondary education. In school districts that implement middle schools, high schools begin at ninth grade, while in districts that adhere to a junior high school model, high school typically begins at 10th grade (but may also begin at ninth grade). Adult education is typically considered to be education for non-college students aged 18 and above. However, students as young as 16 may be enrolled in adult education programs in many states. As we begin our discussion of careers in middle elementary grades and beyond, remember that it is important to understand how various schools and school districts of interest to you are organized. If you are considering a career in elementary or secondary education, knowing which grade levels are located in which schools might be helpful in your career exploration and planning (e.g., if I want to teach in sixth grade, will that be in an elementary school or a middle school?).

Human Development for Teachers

This chapter covers careers that serve students across a very wide range of ages. It is apparent that the time between middle childhood (about 8 years old) and adulthood is a period of dramatic physical, social, emotional, and psychological development. This dramatic development happens as humans move from the life of childhood to adulthood, with its responsibilities. A teacher in any given classroom at any given grade level will typically observe only those developmental milestones, developmental tasks, developmental strengths, and developmental barriers that are relevant to her or his students for as long as she or he is their teacher. However, within this broad age range a student's development at any point is not only influenced by prior history, including opportunities and challenges, but is also certain to influence subsequent development as the student moves on from one classroom to another and one educational level to another. The development of an individual is unique and dependent on hereditary and environmental influences, as well as on past experiences and future potential. Underpinning this variety of individual developmental pathways, there is also a pattern of developmental progression that applies to most humans. For all of these reasons, a solid grounding in human development across the full age spectrum of childhood, adolescence, and adulthood will be a great benefit for teachers as they work to maximize the learning of all their students.

A Brief Primer on Concepts Important for Teachers

While it seems reasonable to assume that knowledge of human development is important for teachers at any level, it is equally reasonable to wonder exactly how a comprehensive knowledge of development might enhance a teacher's skills. The previous section described several concepts that you have encountered during your study of human development. Why might these concepts be useful for teachers? What are some of the specific applications of developmental theory that can help teachers better serve their students?

Milestones

Developmental milestones are usually a large part of our understanding of early childhood, but milestones have relevance throughout development. Every individual reaches a specific milestone at an age that reflects his or her personal developmental timetable. However, research demonstrates that all humans achieve a series of milestones throughout life, just not necessarily at the same chronological age. One of many examples of human development theory that incorporate the concept of milestones is Loevinger's (1976) model of development. His work describes seven stages of human development from toddlerhood to early adulthood, and each stage is characterized by distinct developmental milestones. For example, rarely earlier than middle childhood, individuals may enter the Conscientious Stage, at which point they will attain the milestones of (a) recognizing that other people have their own internal interests and opinions and (b) realizing and appreciating that others have viewpoints different from their own. To a teacher, achieving these developmental milestones signals that a student has developed the ability to engage independently in student-directed dialogue, critical analyses of source materials, and other areas of critical thinking. Students in a single classroom might achieve this milestone at different points during a school year, and shaping classroom activities to meet the developmental needs of students can be informed by understanding developmental milestones. Elementary school students may be frustrated by tasks that require critical judgment and analysis if they have not achieved the associated milestones.

Tasks

Similar to milestones, developmental tasks are also usually described as parts of stages of development. The most familiar models that include developmental tasks are Havighurst (1972) and Erikson (1964, 1968). Both of these prolific writers on human development have proposed stages that cover a broad age range of development and specify tasks that must be accomplished for a healthy transition through any given stage. Erikson's model of development, perhaps the most familiar to students of human development, proposes eight phases of development from infancy to old age. According to Erikson, in each stage there is one overriding developmental task that must be accomplished for healthy progression to the next stage of development. For example, for elementary schoolchildren, the stage of industry vs. inferiority comes to the forefront. In this stage, children grapple with the task of becoming competent workers, learning to complete tasks with some independence, and succeeding with work responsibilities. Erikson says that if this task is not successfully mastered, children develop a sense of inferiority or feelings of inadequacy concerning whatever type of work is present during this phase (e.g., academics, helping the family, self-care). For the elementary schoolteacher, it is particularly important to understand which children feel unsuccessful in coping with this developmental task. Children who are feeling inferior or inadequate in their academic work may also become disruptive and uninterested in academic activities and assignments. A solid understanding of the need to successfully master this developmental task will lead teachers to work with individual students to find assignments that are not frustrating signs of inferiority but are sufficiently challenging that the student feels a sense of competence in completing the tasks. Similarly, in middle adulthood, a time when many people might enroll in adult education classes, the stage of generativity vs. stagnation presents the primary developmental task. According to Erikson, people in this age range are concerned with social responsibility and a sense of productivity and accomplishment. Those who have lost a job, been laid off, or desire to break out of a dead-end job may take adult education classes to learn skills leading to jobs that allow them to be a meaningful contributor to their own lives, their families, and their communities. In the absence of a sense of generativity, or feeling like a productive contributor to society, a feeling of stagnation and lack of meaning leads to dissatisfaction with the relative lack of productivity. In general it is best to remember that no matter their age, all students are rarely purposefully disruptive or disengaged for no reason at all, but some who feel completely inadequate or overwhelmed by their circumstances may find such behavior a useful distraction from their feelings of inadequacy.

Strengths and Barriers

It is best to think about these two developmental concepts as two closely intertwined influences on human development. The words themselves are self-explanatory. Poverty, for example, is clearly a barrier to successful, healthy development. Children and families living in poverty face many challenges. If families cannot afford housing, particularly housing in safe neighborhoods, unstable housing leads to chronic moves from one place to another and perhaps one school to another. Poor families must sometimes shop in neighborhoods that lack healthy food choices like fresh fruits and vegetables (i.e., food deserts). If so, these families and their children may consume an unhealthy diet that can lead to health problems (e.g., obesity, diabetes). Adults in low-wage, unpredictable shift work may struggle to attend evening classes that can help them upgrade their skills.

Barriers can sometimes be overcome by strengths in an individual or in a neighborhood, or perhaps in a systemic reform. A parent may find a neighbor with a car, for example, and negotiate weekly trips to a supermarket with healthy food in return for babysitting for the neighbor one evening a week. A community might seek to host a farmers market once a week in the neighborhood to gain access to fresh food. A school system might provide evening and Saturday school to help students of all ages catch up and complete schoolwork that was missed due to multiple school changes or lack of successful school completion.

An understanding of the dual roles of strengths and barriers may be the best information that teachers can use to support the effective learning and development of all students. Unfortunately, a deficit perspective has been the primary approach among some helping professions to students, families, and communities experiencing significant barriers of racism, classism, poverty, community disorder, mental health challenges, low motivation, and low levels of school engagement. That mindset can lead to beliefs that students, families, and communities must be "saved" by professionals, as they are not able to help themselves. Fortunately, in a number of professions, including the preparation of teachers, the deficit perspective has been supplanted by a strengths perspective. This perspective recognizes that every individual, family, and/or community has competencies and resources that support positive development but may encounter barriers blocking the expression of those strengths. The goal of educators is to identify and build upon student strengths in order to support learning. Understanding barriers that students face may help teachers identify strengths that may otherwise be masked. The student of any age who must miss school to care for other family members may be very interested in school but bound by a sense of obligation to put the needs of the family first. Helping the family find child care or home care resources or providing schoolwork that can be done at home are only two responses from a teacher who understands the role of both strengths and barriers. This strengths and barriers perspective is captured in what is known as the transactional model of development (Sameroff, 2009), which is the leading explanation today for understanding healthy development. The transactional model is an essential part of your study of human development, and you are probably familiar by now with this theoretical perspective. Think carefully about how this important body of knowledge can guide the work of education professionals.

Overview of Job Types

When we consider careers in teaching, the job that typically comes to mind is teaching in a traditional public school in a K–12 education system. However, teachers work in a variety of educational settings. The type of school in which you decide to teach will have an impact on how you feel about your teaching career and how successful you will be. From public schools (including magnet schools and charter schools) to private schools (including full-time boarding schools) every classroom setting has its own unique benefits and challenges. Deciding where you want to begin your teaching career is a very important element of the decision to become a teacher.

Where Might I Work?

- **Public school:** Open to everyone who lives in the area of service.
- **Magnet school:** Subcategory of public schools; specialized settings that emphasize a particular area of study.
- **Charter school:** Publicly funded school that is semi-independent of the school district.
- **Private school:** Schools not funded or operated by federal, state, or local governments.

Public Schools

Public schools are universal, which means they are available to everyone. By definition public schools must provide an education to everyone who lives in their area of service. For adult education that might mean anyone who lives in the city or county in which the school is located. For K–12, a public school may admit students from a local community or across the entire district. Public schools are funded and administered by a local school district. However, they are also guided by decisions made by either the federal or state department of education.

Throughout the country, the need for teachers varies by region, grade level and subject matter. Thus one important decision when thinking about a teaching career in public education is determining where jobs are available. For example, schools in poor areas and in sparsely populated rural areas are more often in greater need of teachers in comparison to suburban and affluent areas. However, public school teaching jobs may not be plentiful in one specific school district, subject area, or geographic region. Wherever a job might be located, there are unique benefits available to public schoolteachers. Teaching in a public school offers a measure of job security. Most states have laws that provide tenure after a set amount of years worked to teachers who perform well. Tenure prevents public school-teachers from being fired without just cause and due process. Thus, while it does not guarantee a job, tenure does provide some security, a reward for those who are excellent teachers.

Magnet Schools

Most public school districts in the United States contain subsets of particular types of schools. Magnet schools are one subcategory of public schools. They are highly specialized educational settings that typically emphasize a particular area of study (e.g., STEM careers, technology, performing arts). Magnet schools function under the same laws and policies as traditional schools and may be found in non-traditional settings (e.g., in a downtown commercial building for a business magnet high school) or within an existing traditional school (e.g., school-within-a-school). Teachers who have a particular interest or a hobby that aligns with a magnet school may find such a setting especially satisfying as a career choice.

Charter Schools

Charter schools are publicly funded public schools that operate semi-independently of the school district in which they exist. These schools have increased autonomy from school district regulations and policies. However, they must follow federal laws that cover equal rights, equal access, and non-discrimination. Charter schools are usually founded by entrepreneurs, and they must provide a specific mission that defines their purpose. The mission forms the schools' "charter" or contract between the school's founders and the school's sponsors (usually the board of education for that state or community). The charter specifies the school's programs of study, admissions criteria, employment guidelines, and academic assessments. In exchange for greater autonomy from the local school district, a charter school is subject to periodic performance reviews and may be closed for failing to meet agreed-upon outcomes. If a charter school closes, the school district is under no mandate to provide jobs in regular public schools for the teachers at the charter school. Schools may be located in non-traditional settings (e.g., churches, industrial buildings), surplus public school buildings, existing schools as a school-within-a-school, or new buildings built by the school founders. Charter schools are available as a choice for families rather than by assignment from a school district. For teachers, charter schools may provide more flexibility and choice in curriculum and classroom management but less job security.

Private Schools

Private schools, which are not funded or operated by federal, state, or local governments, offer education ranging from Pre-K to adult education. Private schools come in a variety of formats, including religious or parochial schools, local neighborhood schools, away-from-home boarding schools, and military schools. Private schools charge tuition and typically use a selective admissions process. The price of attendance often determines the diversity (economic, cultural, racial, etc.) of the student body, although private schools may offer scholarships to students with financial need. Because private schools are not paid for by public tax dollars, they are not subject to the regulations that govern public schools, and government agencies wield less power over day-to-day administration. For example, curriculum and instruction is not controlled by government or school district administrators, and therefore teachers have more involvement in decision making. Teachers often get to select the materials that they use. Some private schools, known as parochial schools, provide religious instruction along with academics and are aligned with a church, synagogue, mosque, or other religious institution. In private schools generally, instructional decisions overall are based on school need, school vision, and staff opinion; many private schools also incorporate parents in the instructional decision-making process.

Unlike public schools, private schools rarely offer teacher tenure as a specific policy, meaning that job security is not a future possibility as a matter of employment. Private school teachers also generally earn less than their public school counterparts, with teachers at parochial schools at the lowest end of the salary range. However, teachers in private schools may not be required to have certifications or specific degrees to teach in their subject areas, meaning that you may be able to become a teacher in a private school more quickly than is possible in a public school. Though similarities exist between public and private schools, the distinctions among the various types of schools that exist will influence your thinking as you consider a career in teaching.

Teacher Certification

All teachers must demonstrate some manner of competence before joining the profession. On one hand are private schools: these may not require formal certification but instead leave the assessment of competence to the individual school. On the other hand, in public education, all teachers are required to be licensed. Generally, the field refers to this process as licensure, certification, or credentialing. Teachers can be licensed by grade level (e.g., elementary, adult basic education, secondary), by subject matter, or by some kind of specialization (e.g., reading, special education, English as a second language). Specialist certification generally requires some teaching experience as a prerequisite. Rules for certification or licensure are not uniform; state governments all have some sort of education oversight agency that includes setting standards for teacher certification. Thus, for anyone thinking about becoming a teacher, it is vital to consider the state in which you plan to teach.

All states have the common requirements of the completion of a bachelor's degree and a standardized test to demonstrate subject competency and mastery of basic skills. Undergraduate teacher preparation programs to teach in elementary school generally combine a broad liberal education base with professional studies, training in pedagogy, and diverse field experiences. Coursework most often consists of a base of instruction in humanities, fine arts, sciences, and social sciences; knowledge and skills for teachers, including classroom management, assessment, and technology; and an exploration of contemporary pedagogy (the art and science of teaching). Fieldwork involves classroom observation, student teaching, or an education internship.

The requirements for teacher licensure in secondary schools are somewhat similar but again vary by state. Typically a prospective secondary level teacher must major in an academic subject and also complete requirements for the teaching credential. The coursework, similar to preparation for elementary education, covers subject matter courses, pedagogy, and skills for teachers. The primary difference typically between elementary and secondary education preparation in many instances is the emphasis on coursework in the specific subject matter that the prospective teacher intends to teach.

Alternative Teacher Certification

In addition to completing an academic degree in teacher preparation, many states offer some kind of alternative teacher certification program. These non-traditional teacher preparation programs are designed for individuals who have not completed a formal teacher preparation program at an accredited college or university but wish to become certified teachers. Alternatively certified teachers typically have already completed a bachelor's degree and complete an alternative certification program while teaching full-time. There are a number of pathways that exist at the state level as well as a number of nationally recognized programs.

Teach for America is one of the most widely recognized paths to teacher certification. It requires, as do all programs, a bachelor's degree. After completion of the degree, those accepted into the program attend an intensive summer training program to prepare for their teaching assignment. Details vary by region, but typically participants attend a five-day regional introduction, a five-to-seven week residential institute, including teaching summer school, and one to two weeks of regional orientation. Subsequently, graduates of the program are placed as full-time teachers in public schools in urban or rural areas that are generally difficult for districts to staff with traditionally trained teachers. Because they are considered nontraditional teachers, in most (but not all) states Teach for America graduates are required to complete additional coursework while they are teaching in order to become certified. The program tries to place graduates in schools with other Teach for America graduates, where they serve for two years.

Alternative certification programs vary widely by region, but these programs retain several similarities. They often require the new teachers to enroll in traditional teacher preparation coursework while they teach. Their initial teaching credential is thus a preliminary or transitional certification. Some of these concurrent programs lead ultimately to a Masters' degree in teaching. Alternative programs often require the new teacher to be matched with a mentor teacher who is given time to observe, confer with, and evaluate the new teacher. It is incumbent upon anyone considering becoming a teacher through an alternative pathway to investigate state regulations and opportunities that govern these programs.

Why Teaching?

This chapter has provided information about teaching in a variety of education settings, constraints that might influence students in these settings as well as those preparing to become teachers in these settings, and several ways to become a teacher in these settings.

All this information should play an important role in the decision-making process for those considering teaching in K–12 or adult education. Deciding on a future career is never an easy decision, but for the majority of professional educators in the field today, teaching was the right decision. This chapter will close with an interview with one such professional educator.

Mrs. Johnson's Interview

Mrs. Johnson (not her real name) has been a teacher for the past 25 years. She has had a long and varied career as a professional educator in a variety of settings. She began her career right out of college, with a Bachelor's degree, in a private school teaching a combined early elementary (first through third grade) classroom. She enjoyed the students very much, and found the combined classroom challenging but very good for her students. Older students who were struggling had the opportunity to move more slowly, and younger children had the opportunity to move as quickly as their effort and ability dictated. She worked in this school for six years, but was finally not able to continue because the salary was insufficient for her needs as she grew from a recent college graduate into full adulthood.

She was offered a position in a federally funded adult education program, where she was hired to teach GED and adult basic education courses. This was a complete shift in age and grade level, but she looked forward to the challenge. She stated that she very much enjoyed working with adult students who had taken a wrong turn in life and wished to get back on track. She was very, very impressed with the level of motivation that all of her students displayed, while at the same time she was often dismayed by their limited academic attainment. She had several students during that time who read only as well as her former early elementary students. However, the job lasted only four years, ending when the federal funding ran out and the program was eliminated.

When this job ended she decided to enter the public school system in her city. Her school district offered an alternative education pathway that was specifically designed to serve teachers who had worked in the now-defunct federal program. With very strong references from her former program director and federal monitor, she applied to a local university. Its program was able to secure for her a preliminary teaching credential for elementary education and enroll her in the Masters of education program. At the time of this interview, she had been teaching in the public schools in her city in third and fifth grades at various times for the past 15 years.

Mrs. Johnson is quite happy with her final career choice. She states that working in public schools provides a better salary and much more job security than her prior teaching jobs. As the first in her family to attend college, she is grateful and sometimes surprised to now have a Master's degree. She has been able to offer both financial help and professional guidance to her younger sibling, who is a lecturer at a local community college. Mrs. Johnson's pathway may not be the best path for everyone looking into becoming a teacher, but it led her to sample teaching at many levels of education and settle into the career of her choice.

Career Specifics

We now turn to the question of what characteristics are also important for people who work as professional educators (see Table 4.1). As Socrates famously said, "Education is the kindling of a flame, not the filling of a vessel." Most importantly for this discussion,

Table 4.1 A Good Teacher

Personal Characteristics
- Passion for the practice of teaching.
- A social disposition to sustain caring, genuine relationships.
- Self-knowledge.

Professional Characteristics
- A solid grounding in pedagogy, or the theory and practice of education.
- A foundational knowledge base of human development and learning.
- Command of the specific subject matter to be taught.
- Valuing diversity.
- Self-knowledge.
- Teaching for social justice.

teachers (with parents) carry the responsibility to kindle the flame rather than falling into a perhaps easier task of filling the vessel. What are the best characteristics for people who will take up this formidable responsibility and succeed in igniting the love for learning in their students?

Personal Characteristics

Although there are certainly successful teachers who have come from other professions, it is probably unwise to initially think of a teaching career as a back-up plan. For example, a college student might think "If I can't get a job or a start-up opportunity of my own in technology, I can always teach high school physical science." That is a likely path to a very unsatisfying career or a surprisingly brief time in a job that "just didn't work out." The foundational quality for anyone considering a teaching career must be a genuine passion for the practice of teaching (Moè, 2016). Passion for teaching is often defined as a strong preference for an activity that you believe is important and something worthy of time and energy. At its most fully realized, the passion for teaching is internalized into your identity (Vallerand et al., 2003). This passion might be evident as early as childhood, or may come later in life after another successful career or an intense search for personal and professional fulfillment.

Teaching is simultaneously extremely challenging and extraordinarily satisfying. It requires a unique desire to enthusiastically move forward every student who enters the classroom, even while understanding that many contributors to a student's learning and healthy development may fall beyond the reach of the teacher and the classroom. Teachers are in an enviable position to celebrate successes with their students, provide guidance that sets students of any age on an upward life trajectory, and offer support to students facing one of any number of life's inevitable challenges and defeats. But a passion for education cannot live solely in the mind of the teacher, or it is of little use for the student. The passionate teacher has a strong desire to innovate and move his or her own practice forward. "We have always done it like this" is not a phrase that guides the work of the passionate teacher. Learning from the past is an important responsibility for any educated person, but teachers should retain historical teaching practices only if those practices are useful for their students. Passionate teachers are eager to learn new, proven practices; to improve their own skills continuously; and to encourage their own students to be lifelong learners and critical thinkers. Passionate teachers are determined to create unique, innovative, valuable learning experiences for their students, and they are eager to learn and grow throughout their lifetimes in order to succeed in that undertaking (Thurlings, Evers, & Vermeulen, 2015).

People who thrive in teaching are also those who have a social predisposition to sustain caring, genuine relationships with students, parents, the community, and their school colleagues (Noddings, 1992). Interpersonal relationships are indispensable to the successful teacher. Although most teachers operate individually as the only education professional in a classroom of students, the interpersonal relationships they must build with students, families, and colleagues set the tone for both career satisfaction and student success. It is the teacher's relationships with his or her students that will best inspire students to learn, and the relationships with colleagues will stimulate schoolwide innovation, progress, and the creation of a positive culture for teachers and students alike. The passion for education and the propensity for developing and sustaining authentic, caring relationships are two of the three primary personal characteristics that define teachers who are both successful and joyful.

Another personal characteristic that is vital to the successful teacher is self-knowledge (Allen, Webb, & Matthews, 2016). A person considering teaching as a career must think first about his or her own vision of education, of the self, and the role of the self in the field of education. What is education? What is the purpose of education? What is the role of the teacher in the lives of his or her students? Each of these questions can have one of several answers. Although there is some consensus, a personal answer to any of these questions requires reflection. Thus, someone who is thinking of teaching must have a disposition toward reflection. How passionate am I about becoming a teacher? How eager am I to develop and sustain a network of personal relationships among my colleagues at my school? Answers to any and all of these questions will guide every decision that a teacher is likely to make and may help the person thinking of a career in teaching to make the decision one way or the other. You may never settle on a definitive answer to any of these questions, but by reflecting on these philosophies of life, of self, of teaching, of work, you learn a lot about yourself. This process of reflection for the person thinking of teaching will aid in the decision as to whether teaching is the right career choice at this point in life.

Professional Characteristics

To enjoy a successful career in teaching, there are several characteristics of a professional educator that are essential. If you are thinking of teaching, reflecting on these essential characteristics will be a vital part of the decision making.

Most importantly, successful teachers are in command of their subject matter (Davis, Petish, & Smithey, 2006). The content of this subject matter in elementary, secondary, and adult education is similar in some ways and very different in others. All teachers must have a solid grounding in pedagogy, or the theory and practice of education, which concerns the study of how best to teach. As well, all teachers must be well versed in a foundational knowledge base of human development and learning; students with a major in child or human development are already developing this knowledge base. For those considering a teaching career, the decision includes the level of interest in engaging these various bodies of knowledge.

A successful teacher must be in command of the specific subject matter to be taught (Darling-Hammond & Bransford, 2005). For example, a math teacher is only as successful as the knowledge base he or she commands. Providing inaccurate material and information is not only bad teaching but also genuinely damaging to students. However, subject matter demands are dramatically different across the elementary, secondary, and adult education levels of instruction. Elementary schoolteachers typically provide instruction across a broad range of subject matter, while secondary and adult education teachers specialize in a single subject (math, history, biology, English, etc.). Elementary schoolteachers are typically more likely to master specific information about the teaching of reading, an important task that elementary school students must master. Secondary schoolteachers, in contrast, are typically more likely to orient toward preparing their students for higher education. Adult education teachers typically have a greater knowledge base in the application of classroom subject matter to professional advancement or personal development. Whatever the subject matter or grade level expectations, the decision to become a teacher must include a consideration of the absolute necessity to master several important areas of knowledge. Further, understanding the similarities and differences of the necessary knowledge base for teachers at different grade levels of instruction may guide someone thinking of a career in teaching to the most comfortable level of teaching.

The study of pedagogy will provide a broad repertoire of teaching and guiding strategies that stimulate student learning, motivation, and achievement. A willingness to engage in the study of pedagogy precedes the actual preparation to become a teacher. In order to become a teacher, you must be enthusiastic about learning the art and science of teaching, guiding, and drawing out students so that they become successful learners. Those who decide to become teachers will have a solid grounding in pedagogy through a teacher training program. Those who are thinking of teaching must consider their level of interest and enthusiasm for this vital subject matter.

Diversity

As the preceding discussion may have forewarned you, teachers have to effectively and positively provide the best education possible for all children, and every classroom will have a broad diversity of students—and this diversity includes cultural, language, ethnic, racial, economic, and gender diversity. Every classroom will also include students with a variety of special needs. Make no mistake about it: if you want to become a teacher you will have to be aware of, sensitive to, and encouraging of students from a broad variety of backgrounds and circumstances. No matter what region of the country you plan to work or what level of education you will teach, you will have students from many different backgrounds and circumstances in your classroom.

One of the most important tasks for every teacher is developing a classroom environment and curriculum that are responsive to all students. For everyone thinking of teaching, the necessity to become both culturally aware and self-aware is foundational. Everyone has unconscious beliefs and misconceptions—stereotypes—about those who are different from themselves. Stereotypes are exaggerated or distorted beliefs presumed to be truth about everyone in a given group. Such generalizations do not acknowledge individual differences within a stereotyped group. Women are poor at math; men are violent; poor people are lazy; these are but a few of many common gender, racial, and socioeconomic stereotypes that will compromise effectiveness for teachers and damage students in today's classrooms.

Therefore, as you think about teaching as a career, realize that you must develop a deep understanding and appreciation for the backgrounds and cultures of people unlike yourself. The starting point for this journey will require that you look inward to seek out and acknowledge your own unconscious stereotypes about those who are different from you. These unconscious or *implicit* beliefs can be very powerful in shaping behavior, and some behavior will disadvantage students in your classroom who are members of groups that are stereotyped. Research over the past four decades indicates that teachers are generally more positive in speech that is directed toward European American children than toward ethnic minority children (Tenenbaum & Ruck, 2007). For example, teachers who hold expectations that students of some racial groups are not intelligent are more likely to pass over them in class discussions or give them less time to answer questions. Such behavior becomes a self-fulfilling prophecy because it limits these students' opportunities to learn and thus depresses their achievement. A very famous experiment conducted in the 1960s (Rosenthal & Jacobson, 1968) suggested that teacher beliefs might have a lasting effect on student learning, both negative and positive, but those effects were reduced to virtually zero when teachers took time to get to know their students. The most successful teachers are those who understand, respect, and value the diverse cultures and circumstances of each of their students.

Social Justice

A consideration of classroom diversity must be accompanied by a consideration of social justice. Consistent with the realization that good teachers understand, respect, and value diversity in the classroom and society, excellent teaching occurs in democratic classrooms that incorporate social justice principles. Teachers are change agents in the lives of students, as teachers encourage and guide students to achieve to their maximum potential. This perspective of teacher as change agent also challenges teachers to think critically about social justice issues.

Social justice is represented in the view that everyone deserves equal rights and opportunities. Seeking social justice is the process of pursuing fair and equitable economic, political, educational, and social ends by working together and organizing for the good of all. In the classroom, teaching for social justice involves inspiring students to think deeply and question the world inside and outside the classroom. Teachers create opportunities for their students to think about and come to understand social justice by drawing direct connections from the life and curriculum inside the classroom to real-world issues in their own lives and communities. Regardless of the level of education, from elementary to adult education, all students benefit from classrooms that prepare them to build a more equitable, multicultural society, and become active and effective global citizens.

Ethics

As professionals, teachers have a responsibility to conduct themselves in an ethical manner. As professionals who work with children, teachers must take ethical behavior as a cornerstone of their practice. Teachers are represented by a number of professional organizations, each of which has a statement of ethical practice. The Association of American Educators, for example, a professional organization that focuses on K–12 student achievement, has a code of ethics consisting of four principles that call for understanding teaching as a position of public trust. The principles also define successful teaching as not only supporting the progress of each student toward personal potential, but also toward becoming a citizen of the greater community (AAE, 2016).

The National Education Association, one of the largest professional organizations in the country for K–12 educators, has a well-formulated code of ethics comprising two primary principles. One explains ethical conduct with students and calls on educators to strive to help each student realize his or her potential as a worthy and effective member of society. The other defines ethical conduct within the profession and addresses raising professional standards, responsibly exercising professional judgment, and preventing educational practice by unqualified persons (NEA, 1975). In the field of adult education, the American Association for Adult and Continuing Education has a vision statement that spells out ethical behavior for professionals in adult education. The statement "envision[s] a more humane world made possible by the diverse practice of our members in helping adults acquire the knowledge, skills and values needed to lead productive and satisfying lives" (AAACE, 2013, n.p.). In general, the expectation for ethical teacher conduct at all levels of education is a part of the foundational documents of all of the various professional organizations. These documents generally concur on two basic ideas: the teaching profession is a public good that carries with it major responsibilities to work for the best interests of students, and professionals must work continuously for improvement and guard against any person or personal behavior that would do harm to students or cast the profession in a negative light.

Summary

This chapter presented information about teaching elementary, secondary, and adult education. Both public and private school settings were presented. The qualifications and requirements for the various levels of education were discussed, as were personal characteristics and ethics.

Reflective Questions

1. What is the best way that colleges and universities can prepare teachers?
2. Is the opportunity for alternative certification of teachers a good idea?
3. How do these two areas differ in the preparation of teachers: a sound grounding in subject matter and a sound grounding in child and adolescent development?

Is This Right for You?

Although teaching can be satisfying, it is also very challenging. A passion for teaching can sustain you. Teachers must be patient, flexible, and very ethical. As noted previously, teachers must teach all of their students, who may have varied levels of knowledge and skill. Teachers must also want to keep learning and be students themselves, as new techniques are always being developed and proven as best practice. Additionally, teachers must know how to build relationships with their students and their students' families. Most important, though, is self-knowledge and reflection. A good teacher knows himself or herself well and recognizes the filter through which he or she views the world. A good teacher recognizes his or her own cultural biases and worldview.

References

Allen, M., Webb, A., & Matthews, C. (2016). Adaptive teaching in STEM: Characteristics for effectiveness. *Theory into Practice, 55*, 217–224.

American Association for Adult and Continuing Education (2013). Retrieved from www.aaace.org/?page=WhoWeAre

Association of American Educators (2016). *Code of ethics for educators.* Retrieved from www. aaeteachers.org/index.php/about-us/aae-code-of-ethics

Darling-Hammond, L., & Bransford, J. (Eds.). (2005). *Preparing teachers for a changing world.* National Academy of Education Committee on Teacher Education. San Francisco: Jossey-Bass.

Davis, E. A., Petish, D., & Smithey, J. (2006). Challenges new science teachers face. *Review of Educational Research, 76,* 607–651.

Erikson, E. (1964). *Childhood and society* (2nd ed.). New York: Norton.

Erikson, E. (1968). *Identity, youth, and crisis.* New York: Norton.

Havighurst, R. (1972). *Developmental tasks and education.* New York: D. McKay Co.

Loevinger, J. (1976). *Ego development: Conceptions and theories.* San Francisco: Jossey-Bass.

Moè, A. (2016). Harmonious passion and its relationship with teacher well-being. *Teaching and Teacher Education, 59,* 431–437.

National Education Association (1975). *Code of ethics.* Retrieved from www.nea.org/home/30442. htm

Noddings, N. (1992). *The challenge to care in schools.* New York: Teachers College Press.

Rosenthal, R., & Jacobson, L. (1968). *Pygmalion in the classroom: Teacher expectation and pupils' intellectual development.* New York: Holt, Rinehart & Winston.

Sameroff, A. (2009). *The transactional model of development: How children and contexts shape each other.* Washington, DC: American Psychological Association.

Tenenbaum, H., & Ruck, M. (2007). Are teachers' expectations different for racial minority than for European American students? A meta-analysis. *Journal of Educational Psychology, 99,* 253–273.

Thurlings, M., Evers, A., & Vermeulen, M. (2015). Toward a model of explaining teachers' innovative behavior: A literature review. *Review of Educational Research, 85,* 430–471.

Vallerand, R., Mageau, G., Ratelle, C., Léonard, M., Blanchard, C., Koestner, R., . . . Marsolais, J. (2003). On obsessive and harmonious passion. *Journal of Personality and Social Psychology, 85,* 756–767.

Chapter 5

Educational Leaders and Educational Agencies
Pre-K Through 12th Grade

The careers in this chapter are related to Pre-K through 12th grade education leadership, but they do not include the principal or other leaders located directly in the school. The leaders discussed in this chapter are found in educational agencies outside of the school itself that lead on-site educators who directly impact children and their families. For instance, the schools may be gathered together in a school district with a superintendent as a leader for all schools in the particular district. Additionally, there may be city, county, state, and national educational agencies with leaders and personnel who all support the education that proceeds in Pre-K through 12th grade schools. These leaders do planning, fundraising, curriculum development, monitoring and evaluation, and perform other duties related to leading the schools. Most of the educational agencies and their jobs are related to governments in some way at some level.

The most common educational leadership positions are located in school districts, county offices, state offices, and national offices. Most of these positions are governmental or public positions. Very few, but some, educational agencies are private or not for profit. These institutions are usually based locally but they may also be located in more than one state. These institutions or agencies usually provide consulting, training, or evaluating services.

To become an educational leader, a person usually begins as a teacher. The next step is usually a director, mentor, or assistant principal. After years in such a position, including additional education and credentialing, it is possible to become an educational leader. For instance, you would get a MA in your discipline, or education, or educational administration. Then you would get an administrative credential for the appropriate position. Some educational administrators obtain a PhD or EdD in their discipline or educational administration. Let us begin our journey with leadership positions in school districts.

Careers With School Districts

School districts are groups of local schools that are managed under the same entity. The manner in which schools are grouped can vary (Cox & Cox, 2010; Niemi & Dyck, 2014). Sometimes all local elementary schools are in one district and other times districts encompass Pre-K through 12th grade schools in a certain geographical area. Districts can also expand and merge at various times (Cox & Cox, 2010). The district superintendent is the main leader or chief executive officer (CEO) of a school district. Superintendents are in charge of all facets of educating the children in their school district, from curriculum and professional development of teachers to physical facilities and buildings. Depending on the size of the district, the superintendent may have assistant or associate superintendents to assist with his or her duties. Positions at the district office are responsible for leading the way, and providing emotional support, educational, training, and financial resources to the schools. The people in these positions find themselves obtaining funds, providing training, structuring learning, conducting evaluations, conducting assessments, and providing vision. Typically, to obtain one of these positions you have to garner more than just a BA in child and adolescent development and some years of experience as a teacher. An MA, PhD, or EdD in educational leadership or curriculum and instruction, or program evaluation, can all help on the road to becoming a superintendent or another position at the district level. Additionally, you will need to obtain the appropriate permits or credentials associated with the position.

The following two interviews are from district superintendents. One is retired and the other is still active. Both are from rural school districts, but from different states. The similarities and differences in their career journeys are fascinating.

Mallory's Interview

Mallory is retired from being a superintendent after 19 years. She has a BS in elementary education, a MS in educational leadership, and a PhD in educational leadership. She keeps busy by teaching at a local university. She spent most of her work life in a rural educational district in Illinois. She describes the job of superintendent as being a system leader who wears a lot of hats and connects all the dots. She says superintendents are business managers, personnel directors, and curriculum directors. They provide support for and give resources to teachers and surrounding communities. They must also get involved in student activities.

Mallory's road to becoming a superintendent was traditional. She wanted to be an educator since her childhood, when she always wanted to play school and be the teacher. She also had a role model, because her maternal grandmother went to college at age 50 and became a teacher. Mallory taught in elementary schools, junior high schools, and high schools. She decided to get an additional degree in educational administration, because a professor mentioned it to her. She was a bit hesitant, because there were very few females in educational administration at the time—but she decided to do it anyway. She enjoyed being an educational leader and held positions as a principal at all three levels; she even took leadership roles in professional associations at the state and national levels. As a leader she saw her job as increasing funding, expanding educational capacity, and getting resources for teachers and students. One highlight of her journey was designing and training many of Illinois' educational administrators through an executive university program.

As for her current family life, her husband was a teacher and coach in addition to an assistant principal and a superintendent. He is now retired, as Mallory is. She feels she was drawn to him because of a similar interest in education and that this has influenced her career journey.

When Mallory began her career, she loved being a teacher—and she still does. It is not really "work" to her. She finds joy in everyday experiences. What she loves about being in the educational field (especially as superintendent) is seeing the success of her students, her teachers, and other staff. She really enjoys connecting students with resources, programs, and opportunities. Additionally, she loves being able to provide service, training, and benefits to faculty and staff members who serve students. She thinks the educational field is the best because it prepares the next generation.

When asked why she thinks she is successful, her humility shows: She mentions perseverance, determination, and intuition. She also says that she has a desire to connect with extraordinary people and best practices in the field. She is extraordinary, too.

Stan's Interview

Stan is currently a superintendent in rural Arizona and is just completing his third year in that role. He came to this position from being a coach/teacher in high school for seven years and then a high school principal for one year. He possesses a BA in organizational development and a MA in educational leadership, and he is currently completing an EdD in educational leadership. His route to being superintendent was shorter than Mallory's route to the same title. This may reflect their different eras or genders.

Stan believes that his early life impacted his career choice. Both of his parents were educators. His mother taught junior high for 22 years and his father was a superintendent of schools for 22 years. In all, his father was in education for 50 years. His father's example and guidance gave him his initial interest in education as a career.

Before Stan became a superintendent, he spent 8 years in private school Pre-K through 12th grade education. He returned to public education when the superintendent position became open. Those 15 years in private school education taught him a lot about finances and business operations. Being a football coach also taught him a lot. He is proud that 15 student-athletes that he coached received college scholarship opportunities and have gone on to live successful lives. The only challenges he sees in being an educator are low pay and the need to relocate for career growth and advancement. However, Stan loves his life and feels blessed.

The personal qualities and experiences that helped Stan succeed began early in life. He has interacted with a wide range of people and cultures. This has helped him enrich his capacity for empathy and understanding. He thinks that playing athletic sports in high school and college increased his competitiveness and drive. He works hard to build relationships and treat everyone with respect. He has developed his people skills over the years. He also believes that he is a hard worker and a self-starter and that these characteristics serve him well.

The General Path

As you can see from these two interviews, the path to superintendency is not uniform. Some of the similarities are starting with teaching and furthering your education. You also have to have leadership ability, skills, and knowledge. Working hard and the ability to multi-task seem to help. Does this career path interest you? Do you believe you have the prerequisite skills and dispositions? There are other educational agencies where one can find a career by starting with child and adolescent development. Most counties and states and our country have educational agencies with leaders. The titles of the leaders vary from coordinators, to directors, to executive directors to presidents and/or superintendents.

Governmental Offices of Education

City, county, state, and federal governments where Pre-K through 12th grade education takes place usually have offices or agencies that support education in their geographical area. Sometimes individual cities have offices of education. More typically, though, counties, states, and the federal government have agencies that support education of 3 year olds to 18 year olds in Pre-K to 12th grade. The agencies have directors and assistant directors and associate directors along all levels and types of education. There are also specialists and others who support their efforts. Grants, taxpayer funds, and sometimes donations support these offices or agencies. At the state level the leader is usually the state superintendent of education. The state superintendent of education has subordinates who focus on specific levels or types of education. Most of the higher-level positions in government education agencies are political positions and the person is voted in by citizens. Sometimes, though, they can be appointed, especially at the state or federal level. In the United States, the highest level of leadership is the federal secretary of education.

There are usually a number of levels and types of education that are the foci of the workers in these agencies. Some workers focus on ECE, elementary education, and secondary education. Others may focus on nutrition, health, and physical education. Other types of education or educational domains are special education, education of children from impoverished families, sports and athletics, and maintenance of educational facilities. Some other typical educational domains are curriculum and instruction, professional development of teachers, program evaluation, and after-school programs. Most of the workers who have careers in these positions have taught at one point along their journey. They also usually further their education and obtain the appropriate credentials. However, they now provide indirect, support services for the educational process. The following interview gives you an example of one of these careers, as Nora works at a county office of education.

Nora's Interview

Nora is a director of school readiness in a large metropolitan county office of education. She has been in the field for more than 30 years. She has a BA in liberal studies, an MA in educational administration, and an EdD in educational leadership. She also has an administrative credential, a multiple subjects credential, and a child development permit. She worked throughout college and graduate school so that she would not have to take out loans.

In her early years her father impressed upon her the importance of education, encouraging her and modeling appropriate behavior in terms of education. She watched as he furthered his education, while working full-time. She also saw a lot of educators and leaders in her family, including teachers and principals. This may be why she graduated high school a year early. However, she started her career journey thinking she would be an architect. It was her mentors and close advisors who noticed her gifts as an educator and encouraged her to go into education. Her mentors have played a valuable role in her career trajectory, as they have guided and encouraged her along the way.

Nora is married, with one daughter. She started out as a teacher and then became a resource teacher and coordinator. She spent some time as an educational specialist before becoming a principal. She had her daughter when she was a principal. Because she believes in the importance of the early years of a child's life, she decided to stay home with her child. She urges women—indeed all parents—to do this if they can afford it, but advises them to stay involved in their field and keep honing their skills. When she made this decision, she was confident that she could return to the workforce at the appropriate time. While at home, she took numerous consulting positions until her daughter went to school and she could return to work full-time, becoming a coordinator and then a director after she received her administrative credential. She has a been a director for 13 years.

The key highlights and turning points along the way have been meeting her mentors, the birth of her daughter, and obtaining her current job. Her mentors first noticed her gift for teaching. Had it not been for them, she would still be an architect. With the birth of her daughter, she left her position as a principal, but was determined to return to work in five or six years. She has no regrets about giving herself, her daughter, and her family that gift of time. Obtaining her current job, director of school readiness, is another highlight. She started on a one-year contract and had to prove herself. Since then, she has grown the number of staff, brought in millions of dollars in grants, and helped many, many people. She is quite proud of her accomplishments in this regard.

One key challenge that impacted her career choice is that her high school counselors were quite discouraging. Because of the support of her family and mentors, she was able to persevere and succeed. For a while, she wanted to be a school counselor to make a difference in the lives of others—but the urging of her mentors to enter education leadership prevailed.

The personal qualities that helped Nora be a success are that she is optimistic, determined, passionate about her work, a planner, and a seeker of excellence at all times. She is also goal-oriented and a life-long learner. The pursuit of excellence and helping people and the community really drive her, especially the pursuit of excellence. One of her favorite quotes is "Autograph your work with excellence."

Nora has advice for potential educational leaders: Always be prepared for opportunities that come your way. In addition, not only does your passion drive you, but it also motivates others to do the work. Also, leaders should create a culture of respect, support for each other, and excellence. This is because people will rise to what leaders do. Leadership is giving back to the community and supporting others, working together to collectively make things happen in the community.

Career Specifics

Characteristics and Abilities

Leading a major agency takes management abilities, vision, and plenty of relevant experience. A leader has to know how to prioritize multiple tasks and responsibilities. Also, the love of working with people is important. Leaders need to be able to work with uncertainty, as well. This is because their positions are usually dependent upon political votes or political appointments and/or temporary grant funds. They also need the same characteristics of a teacher, because that is usually the starting place for their career.

Salary

During the Obama administration, the United States secretary of education made approximately $205,700 a year (Paywizard, 2017). District superintendents make approximately $98,000 to $211,000 depending on where they live and the number of students served (Table 5.1).

Table 5.1 School Superintendent Salaries in the United States

Percentile	Salary
10th Percentile School Superintendent Salary	$98,254
25th Percentile School Superintendent Salary	$123,451
50th Percentile School Superintendent Salary	$151,127
75th Percentile School Superintendent Salary	$182,361
90th Percentile School Superintendent Salary	$210,798

Source: Salary.com (2017)

Ethics

When talking about ethics of educational leaders, let us begin at the top. In the United States the secretary of education has to take an oath (see Figure 5.1). However, the ethical requirements go beyond this oath. The secretary of education has to be accountable to taxpayers and do as the president of the United States requests. He or she has to follow all laws of the land and international agreements between the United States and its allies. As the secretary sets the tone for all education in the country, he or she has to model the most ethical behavior of all at all times.

Other educational leaders have to be ethical, too. For instance, all educational leaders usually belong to a professional organization, much as professors and teachers do, that has requirements for their ethical behavior. For instance, district superintendents have two professional organizations: the National Association of School Superintendents and the American Association of School Administrators (AASA). The latter of these two organizations has specific ethical guidelines for its members that include a preamble and a list of behavior standards. These standards include "implements local, state and national laws" and "commits to serving others above self" (Figure 5.2).

As you can see, educational leaders are held to the highest ethical standards. They set the tone for other educational personnel and their country. Their behavior as leaders sets ripple effects into the education profession as a whole. Because their behavior impacts the education of the nation's children, it should follow the highest ethical standards.

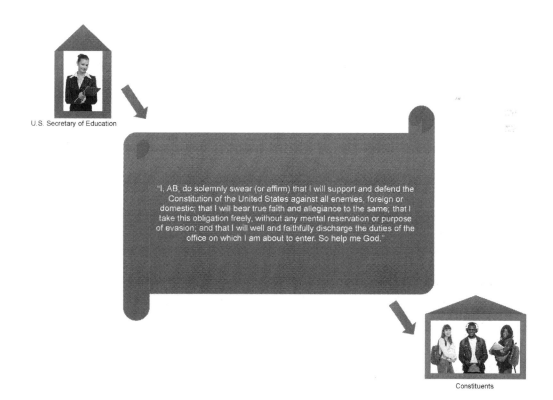

U.S. Secretary of Education

"I, AB, do solemnly swear (or affirm) that I will support and defend the Constitution of the United States against all enemies, foreign or domestic; that I will bear true faith and allegiance to the same; that I take this obligation freely, without any mental reservation or purpose of evasion; and that I will well and faithfully discharge the duties of the office on which I am about to enter. So help me God."

Constituents

Figure 5.1 United States Secretary of Education Oath of Office

Source: Cornell University Law School, Legal Information Institute (1966)

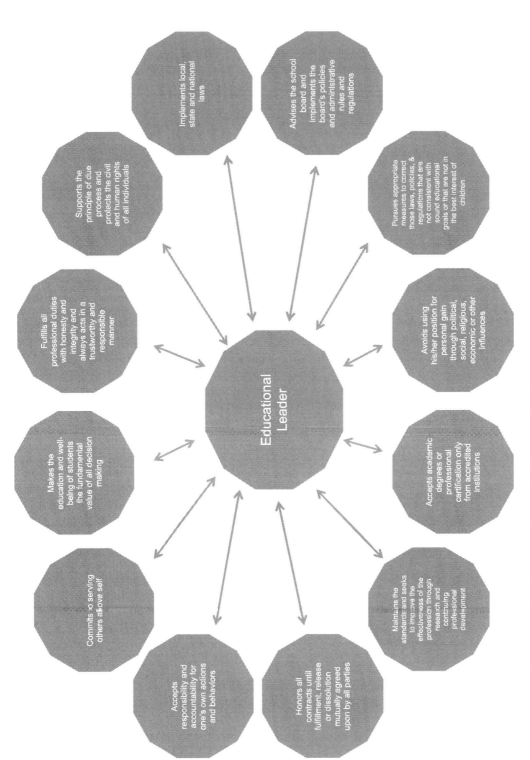

Figure 5.2 Code of Ethics—AASA's Statement of Ethics for Educational Leaders

Source: American Association of School Administrators (2017)

Summary

Educational leaders usually have some experience in the educational system as a teacher and/or principal before taking on a leadership position. These leaders usually work at educational agencies and do not provide direct services to students. Instead, they support students through staff training, program evaluations, and provision of financial resources.

The foremost educational leader in the United States is the federal secretary of education, who is appointed by the president of the United States. At the state level the leaders have titles such as state superintendent of education. Locally, you find positions such as superintendent of a school district or director of a city or county office of education. People who work in these positions usually have many years of experience in the educational system. They must behave in a highly ethical manner, because they support children's education, children's futures, and the future of the country. They provide vision and leadership.

Reflective Questions

1. Most educational leaders have an easygoing temperament and an outgoing, extroverted personality. What are the strengths of this personality type? Can a more introverted and slow-to-warm person be an effective educational leader?
2. Educational leadership positions are usually obtained through a political process. How do you think this impacts leaders' behavior and decisions? How does this impact the education of the country's children?
3. Educational leaders usually begin as teachers in the educational system and then become principals or directors or coordinators. What do you think are the personal characteristics and qualities a person needs to make these transitions?

Is This Right for You?

Being an educational leader of an educational entity is like being a CEO of a company. Educational leaders work many countless hours. They also have a tremendous responsibility: the education of our country's children and the future of our nation. In the author's view, an introvert can lead as well as an extrovert. However, extroverts are usually preferred in leadership positions of all types, including education. This is something you should consider before pursuing an educational leadership position.

In order to obtain a leadership position, you may have to switch positions more than once. This is also a consideration when choosing this career path. For example, Stan moved around the country a number of times before becoming a school district superintendent.

Another consideration before taking an educational leadership position is whether or not you want to provide direct or indirect services to students. In other words, if you love interacting with students on a daily basis, you may want to be a teacher or principal for your entire career. You may become a curriculum coordinator or mentor teacher who still has daily contact with students, but a more indirect influence on students may not be for you. For some educational leaders, leadership is their calling. It is your responsibility to discern which position is optimal for you.

References

American Association of School Administrators. (2017). *AASA Statement of Ethics for Educational Leaders*. Alexandria, VA: Author.

Cornell University Law School, Legal Information Institute. (1966). 5 U.S. Code § 3331—Oath of Office.Ithaca, NY: Author.

Cox, B., & Cox, B. (2010). A decade of results: A case for school district consolidation. *Education*, *131*(1), 83–92.

Niemi, R. G., & Dyck, J. J. (2014). *Guide to state politics and policy*. Los Angeles, CA: Sage Publications.

Paywizard. (2017). Retrieved from http://paywizard.org.

Salary.com. (2017). *School superintendent salaries*. Retrieved from www1.salary.com/School-Superintendent-salary.html

Chapter 6

Educational Consultants and Specialists

The two job titles represented in this chapter represent a variety of positions in a variety of settings. The percentage of work and number of simultaneous jobs also vary. For instance, a consultant may have two or three contracts at once and thereby really be working on a full-time basis. Some consultants, however, prefer to work on a strictly part-time basis. Also, a specialist may work directly for one employer on a full-time or part-time basis. A specialist may also work independently with two or three contracts, using his or her home as a base of operations for full-time or part-time work. Unless a consultant or specialist is employed directly by an employer, they do not know when the next job will happen or from where the next job will come. Some people prefer to work this way, but others want a more stable job. Some people hold the title of consultant or specialist, while working full-time in another job. Being a consultant is really a flexible, part-time job in this case. These two job titles can happen anywhere along a person's career trajectory. Some people choose to alternate between a full-time position with an employer and having a consulting job, depending on what phase of life they are in at the time. Consultants and specialists can have a variety of other job titles, too. To name a few, they can be coaches, evaluators, or mentors. The key takeaway is that this career involves part-time work, contract work, and possible full-time self-employment.

The areas in which you can consult also vary. For instance, you can be a consultant with educational program evaluation or college application preparation (Antonoff, 2012; Sklarow, 2012). You can be a consultant or specialist along certain phases of child and adolescent development. For instance, you can be an infant/toddler specialist or an adolescent specialist. Specializing in this way demonstrates a particular expertise in a specific age range. You can also be an instructional coach/mentor or a tutor. Instructional coaches are sometimes hired full-time by school districts at particular schools or sometimes work on a part-time basis. Instructional coaches/mentors usually focus on one curriculum area such as history, mathematics, English, science, or some other curriculum area (Butler & Votteler, 2016; Eaton, 2015). Tutors usually work part-time, but can sometimes work full-time for a tutoring agency or own a tutoring agency. In general, consultants or specialists have specific and specialized knowledge. They also usually work part-time or on a contract. These elements of their work life distinguish them.

Requirements and Duties as Explained in Literature

Eaton (2015) explains the duties of a TESOL (teacher of English to speakers of other languages) professional who is self-employed. This self-employed person can be a contract employee, freelancer, independent contractor, or consultant. They can even perform all four functions to varying degrees. Duties vary depending on the exact role, as can be seen

Table 6.1 Independent TESOL Professional Duties

	Contract Employee	Freelancer	Independent Contractor	Consultant
Tutoring	Possibly	✔	✔	
Teaching	✔	✔	✔	
Workshops	✔	✔	✔	
Presentations	✔	✔	✔	
Administering exams	✔	✔	✔	
Invigilating exams	✔	✔	✔	
Exam marking	✔	✔	✔	
Writing	✔	✔	✔	
Editing	✔	✔	✔	
Translation	Possibly	✔	✔	
Interpretation	Possibly	✔	✔	
Teacher training	✔	✔	✔	
Recruiter	✔	✔	✔	
Works directly with students or clients	✔	✔	✔	Rarely
Narrow scope of service	✔	✔	✔	
Developing materials	✔	✔	✔	✔
Curriculum development	✔	✔	✔	✔
Program evaluation	Possibly	✔	✔	✔
Accreditor		✔	✔	✔
Broad scope of service				✔
Needs assessment				✔
Environmental scan				✔
Strategic planning				✔
Organizational development				✔
Works almost exclusively with management				✔

Source: Eaton (2015).

in Table 6.1. TESOL professionals can perform a number of duties from tutoring to interpreting to organizational development to program evaluation. These duties can be performed in an endless set of combinations, depending on the role you are playing.

Education and Experience Needed

The education and experience needed to become a specialist or consultant varies with the position. Usually you need Bachelor's and Master's degrees in child and adolescent development or some related field. However, you can start tutoring while in college. This is a common practice for college students who have high grades and good skills in particular subject matter. It is helpful for their peers or younger students and it allows them to make extra money. But, as stated previously, at least a Masters degree is needed for the title of specialist or consultant. Indeed, a doctorate of some kind is helpful for obtaining steady work and increasing your level of pay. Remember that you can also work as a consultant or specialist to supplement income from another full-time job.

In terms of experience, usually you need at least two years of experience in the area where you are consulting or fulfilling the role of specialist. In some cases, a contract or client may require five or more years of experience before you are eligible for completing the work and considered to be credible. You may also need to complete a specialized training program related to your consultant or specialist position. For instance, a tutor may need some procedural or pedagogical training. An evaluator may need statistical and research methods training. A coach or specialist in a particular subject matter needs to keep abreast of what is current in his or her field. A college entrance consultant may require specialized training, in addition to knowing the basics of college entrance exams and college application processes and financing college.

Settings and Duties

Due to the short-term and contractual nature of much of this work, the home office is the place where most of it takes place. Consultants and specialists usually work out of their home. They can get contracts from various nonprofit or educational agencies, and from local, state, and federal governments. Those who have full-time positions may be located within a school district, a college or university, a nonprofit agency, or a government agency. Of course, they can have their own business or work for another for-profit business, such as a tutoring company. Keep in mind that this may not be your only job and that this job title can come at any place in your career.

A consultant's or specialist's duties depends on his or her job at the moment. These professionals usually write reports, observe programs and teachers, train other professionals in the field of education, gather and analyze data, give workshops, and perform other such tasks. Sometimes they teach in a traditional setting. They also attend conferences to keep up-to-date in their field. Additionally, they have to keep writing proposals and bids for contracts.

Their duties can be unpredictable. Each day, each hour brings with it new challenges and unexpected occurrences. One day or one week can look different from the next. One consideration is that there may be periods of few job tasks and duties and there may be times when a flood of job duties make for long days and weeks filled with work.

Real-Life Interviews

Let us now take a look at two real-life stories, Vanessa and Ralph. Vanessa is an infant/toddler specialist in California near the beginning to middle of her career. Ralph is a consultant, an evaluator in Arizona, toward the end of his career. Let us start at the beginning with Vanessa.

Vanessa's Interview

Vanessa is an infant/toddler specialist and a part-time adjunct lecturer at colleges and universities near her home. She has held these positions for three years. She has both a BA and MA in child and adolescent development. Before she became an infant specialist, she was a full-time infant-toddler teacher at a high-quality, university-based child care center for six years. She made the transition to infant specialist to relieve the stress of the full-time position and obtain better hours for parenting her own two young children.

Vanessa believes that her early years influences her career decisions. She wanted to focus on child and adolescent development because her mother was a lover of children. Her mother and father divorced when she was about 6 years age. She was raised by her mother, who cared for, taught, and fostered children. She likes to jokingly call her mother "a collector of children." Her mother's unselfish ways taught her to care for others and love children.

Vanessa's current family situation also influenced her career. She had a full-time position as an infant-toddler teacher in a coveted child care center—a plum job in the field.

However, it was somewhat stressful and she was putting in long hours. So after some specialized training, she decided to work part-time to spend more time with her two young children. That is when she became an infant/toddler specialist and part-time lecturer. She is grateful that she can stay in a field that she loves and make more room for her family.

There have been two major turning points in her career. Vanessa was happy to begin working with a wonderful group of teachers at a quality child care center. This experience helped her to understand children and who the children really are. Another pivotal point was choosing to get some specialized training and leave her well-paying, full-time job.

There have been joys and challenges along her career journey. Vanessa's biggest joy has been having former parents or previous mentees come back and tell her how much what she taught them has made a big difference in their lives. She also is proud of the fact that she was a quality infant/toddler teacher who raised the bar on meeting the needs of children and families. She has had three major challenges. One challenge was believing in her own knowledge and abilities enough to feel confident enough to train and mentor others. One was finding quality care and education for her own children while she was working. The third challenge was taking the risk to leave an excellent full-time position to take on contract and part-time work.

There have been outside influences on Vanessa's career, including friends and family members who have supported and believed in her. Sometimes they pushed her to take advantage of opportunities. Her husband has been really supportive, pushing her to try and do more. She has a tremendous and supportive network of friends and family.

So what exactly are Vanessa's duties? You can see from Figures 6.1 and 6.2 that she has two main job titles: infant/toddler specialist and part-time adjunct lecturer. As a specialist, she follows the policies of the organization that hired her. However, she works for the organization on a part-time contract basis. She trains, coaches, and instructs. She gives relevant feedback. She writes reports and submits other paperwork to her supervisor. She enters information into a database and is observed herself once a year for evaluation purposes.

- Work collaboratively with each organization's administrative staff and contact person to negotiate and implement services.
- Provide training and coaching to assigned sites in accordance to the established policies and procedures.
- Provide instruction and grading for students enrolled for academic credit in accordance with policies.
- Submit all required paperwork in accordance with policies, including but not limited to:

  Timesheets and copies of training participant sign-in sheets submitted weekly.

  Progress reports uploaded to database no later than the 5th of each month. Progress reports describe changes, mplementation, successes, and challenges in both training and coaching activities.

  Local travel reimbursement and other claims monthly to the Regional Office, no later than the 5th of each month.

  Closing paperwork including all academic assignments and grades.

  Report at least monthly to your Regional Coordinator via telephone and/or email on status of training plan(s) and any challenges.

  Training plans for approval using the database.

- Attend regional I/T Specialist meetings (3x/year) and other training events (Advanced Training) as available.
- Participate in a minimum of one observation by your Regional Coordinator each year. Discuss observation and incorporate feedback into the PQ services you provide.

Figure 6.1 Specialist Duties

- Develop teaching strategies on term (semester or quarter) basis.
- Organize, prepare, and revise (as needed) course materials.
- Ensure content level of course materials in exams has been covered in class.
- Design, administer, and grade examination, papers, and projects.
  - Assess student learning through various methods.
  - Incorporate a variety of teaching methodologies within a class.
  - Communicate with students on a regular basis.

Figure 6.2 Adjunct Lecturer Duties

As an instructor in a child development department, Vanessa mainly teaches college-age students. She has to be organized and to vary instruction and assessment strategies. She designs educational materials and communicates regularly with her students. Sometimes she has little time to prepare because class assignments may come only one day before the class starts. In addition, because she is a part-time adjunct instructor, she never knows if she will have any courses to teach the following semester.

Vanessa believes she is successful in her positions because she is able to relate to and connect with people. She is also a forever learner who loves learning new techniques and strategies. She really and truly believes that it takes an entire supportive system to raise children.

Ralph's Interview

Ralph is coming to the close of his career. He has been conducting evaluations for more than 40 years. When asked about his education, he reveals that he has a Doctorate in educational psychology with a focus on statistics and research. This is a field related to child and adolescent development.

Ralph does not see a connection between his family life and his career; he just looked at the available jobs and made career decisions based on availability at times of transition.

He began his career as a professor and completed evaluations at that time. He moved up into high levels of administration, even becoming provost of a university. All the while, he was designing and conducting evaluations. His many years in higher education administration are the highlight of his career. He finds working with a variety of people challenging, but it also brings him great joy. The personal characteristics that make him successful include his sense of humor, dedication, and hard work.

At this point in his career, he works part-time as an evaluator and an adjunct professor. The key is that both positions are part-time and on a contract basis. He teaches online classes, mostly. On any given day, he checks his classes electronically to keep up with messages and assignments, such as discussion boards and exams. He also grades assignments online. He is currently designing an evaluation that examines the retention of rural teachers and administrators, addressing two main issues: Why do some teachers and administrators stay in a rural area? Why do some teachers and administrators leave from rural areas? He is a consultant on this project. He works mostly from home—or anywhere he has access to the internet, such as on the golf course.

Career Specifics

Characteristics and Abilities

A person who is a specialist or consultant needs to have some knowledge and experience in an area that is highly needed, plus the ability to relate to and connect with people. They need to have a salesperson's personality and a network of people who can provide contract leads. They have to be flexible and to accept the uncertainty of this type of profession. Management of time and money are also very important skills to have. Every day is quite variable, as is compensation.

Risks

With all of these choices come some risks, including not having a steady paycheck and needing to purchase your own insurance. In certain circumstances, these risks may well be worth it. In other cases, they may not be.

Salary

The amount of money that you can make as a consultant or specialist varies widely. Eaton (2015) suggests that you consider very carefully how much is needed to pay your bills and living expenses. She uses $50,000 gross salary a year as an example amount to meet living expenses. She also states that you must consider your costs of running a business, such as insurance and other business costs. According to her example, these costs run approximately $4,350 a year. Therefore, one needs to gross around $54,350 a year for the example annual salary. These estimates are more appropriate for states with an average cost of living, such as New Mexico and Indiana.

Ethics

Consultants and specialists fall under a variety of operational guidelines and principles. The general ethical principles mentioned in Chapter 13 of this book surely apply here. However, any professional associations to which a consultant or specialist belongs also has ethical principles to follow. For instance, the American Evaluation Association has a set of ethical principles that can be seen in Figure 6.3. Additionally, the contracts and

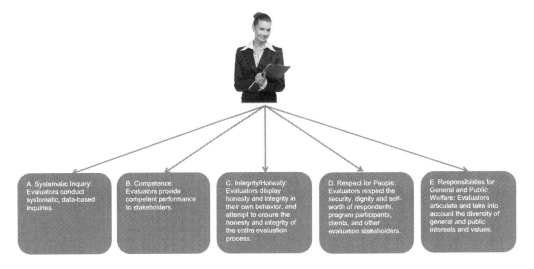

Figure 6.3 AEA Guiding Principles for Evaluators

organizations and businesses that the consultant or specialist works with may have ethical guidelines for them to follow.

Summary

The central theme of this chapter is that of variety. As an educational consultant or educational specialist, there are lots of possibilities and some risks involved. You can have part-time or contract work or be self-employed full-time. You can work one or more part-time jobs or have one or more contracts. You can also vary the areas and age groups that are the focus of your consulting. For instance, you can be a specialist in adolescent internet usage or a college admissions coach. The settings for these jobs often vary widely, but usually involve some sort of home office. You can have these job titles anywhere along your career trajectory; somewhere near the beginning, middle, or end.

However, along with all of these choices come some risks and ethical guidelines to be followed. In certain circumstances, these risks may well be worth it; in others, they may not. The ethical guidelines of a consultant or specialist vary. The varied duties and varied daily schedules of a consultant or specialist just complicate the ethical landscape.

It takes a special set of characteristics and abilities to be a consultant or specialist. The potential for income varies widely. So a tolerance for income fluctuation and variability is a must. You must be somewhat of a risk taker. You must have requisite subject matter knowledge and skills and you must also have management, marketing, and sales skills. Indeed, the characteristics and skills needed to be a successful consultant or specialist vary as wide as the tasks, settings, and income.

Reflective Questions

1. Is there someone in your own life (including yourself) that you think would be a good consultant or specialist?
2. Do you think men or women would be better as a consultant or specialist? List and describe three reasons for your beliefs.
3. Do you think that men or women would be more interested in being a consultant or specialist? Do you think the motives men and women have for starting this career path may be different? List and describe three reasons for your beliefs.

Is This Right for You?

Although this career categorization is the most ambiguous, it may also be the most attractive for some people. Some will be attracted to the flexibility and part-time nature of the career and others the non-restricted income potential. However, this career carries with it a lot of variability and some risks. These are mentioned in the chapter and deserve consideration when determining if this career is right for you. This career would not be right for people who want a steady and predictable paycheck, and a regular and stable schedule. Some people do not tolerate risks well and others are not good salespeople or managers. This career would not be right for them either. This career is right for you if you thrive on variability and can tolerate risk, if you can sell your knowledge and skills to others, and if you can manage your own schedule and flow of income. These types of jobs may be right for you temporarily, along certain phases of your career journey. Maybe the beginning or end of your journey lends itself to being a consultant or specialists. Perhaps you can work as a consultant or specialist while working full or part-time for an employer. After all of these considerations, do you think this career is right for you?

References

Antonoff, S. R. (2012, Winter). *Educational consulting: A focus for the profession.* Retrieved from http://files.eric.ed.gov/fulltext/EJ992742.pdf

Butler, M. S., & Votteler, N. K. (2016). Disequilibrium: An instructional coach's reflection. *Texas Journal of Literacy Education, 4,* 29–36. Retrieved from https://eric.ed.gov/?id=EJ1110859

Eaton, S. E. (2015). *Your career as a successful independent TESL professional.* Paper presented at the meeting of the TESL Canada 2015 Conference, Alberta, Canada, Oct 29-31.

Sklarow, M. H. (2012, Winter). *Educational counseling: Justification to partnership.* Retrieved from http://files.eric.ed.gov/fulltext/EJ992743.pdf

Chapter 7

College and University Positions

Teaching, Researching, Leading, and Providing Service

In this next chapter we are presenting higher education professor and administrative positions that child and adolescent development majors can enter with an advanced degree such as a MA, PhD or EdD. You will learn more about what college and university professors do on their job in order to explore whether this job is right for you. As with most professions in education, the job is different depending on the type of institution and setting and regional location (Bok, 2015). This is the position with which we are most familiar, because this is what we do (or did) for our careers.

There are two main differences in the students that professors teach in higher education when compared to students that attend elementary and secondary education. One difference is higher education is voluntary and not compulsory. In other words, the students go because they choose to obtain a higher education (postsecondary) degree and not because it is mandated by law. The second main difference is that, in most instances, the students are now legally considered to be adults. Yes, the vast majority of college and university students are considered adults by law: They are 18 years of age or older. However, it is important to note that in the field of child and adolescent development, we study people from conception to age 25 years. However, the age of 18 years is a time when many rights and privileges are bestowed upon children. In general and legally, children become adults at age 18.

Some other differences exist between higher, postsecondary education and the compulsory education of the earlier years (Bok, 2015). Teachers usually have more freedom in what they teach and how they teach it (American Association of University Professors, 2009; Meyer, 2012). Students also have more choices in what they choose to study and how they choose to study it. To illustrate the choices that students have, they can learn at a private, nonprofit university or college; a private, for-profit college; a two-year public college; or a four-year public university or college. The choices can be even more complicated, because private and public universities can be different types (Bok, 2015; Chronicle of Higher Education, 2012). Four-year universities and/or colleges may emphasize teaching or research as their main goal or mission. They may also emphasize providing a liberal arts (general) education or providing a focused education on a singular profession or group of professions, such as engineering or medical professions. Moreover, courses can be taught totally in person, totally online, or hybrid, which is a mix of online with some in-person class meetings. Courses can also be taught over distances short or long. For instance, you can live in Texas and take courses from a school in Florida or Pennsylvania. Or you can live in rural New York state and take classes in Manhattan. Students who attend postsecondary colleges or universities have an array of choices.

If you choose to go into one of these higher-education professions, you have several options of workplace settings of which to choose. You can also choose the balance of how much teaching, researching, leading, and providing of service you want for your daily and weekly life (Bok, 2015; Meyer, 2012). For instance, if you work at a teaching two-year community college, you will spend the majority of time teaching with few research responsibilities. In a research-focused university the percentage of time spent researching increases and the time spent teaching decreases. Professors also have to provide service to their workplace, their profession, and their local and global communities. Moreover, professors get the opportunity to lead: for example, they may take a leadership role on a grant project, or manage their colleagues as a chair of the department. They can also further their leadership roles by becoming a director of a program or dean of a college. Typically leadership roles come after years of experience as a professor. Deciding to focus on a college or university position within the field of child and adolescent development gives you a lot of options. However, you must prepare for these opportunities with the appropriate educational preparation and experiences.

Preparing for College and University Positions

Advanced degrees are needed to pursue a college or university position in child and adolescent development (Bok, 2015; Chronicle of Higher Education, 2012). So, if this is your goal, please remember that you will need to obtain at least a MA degree in child and adolescent development or a related field. However, you will have more opportunities and avenues available if you have a doctorate, such as a PhD or EdD. Most professors in the field of child and adolescent development have a PhD in child and adolescent development or applied developmental psychology or educational psychology or another related field. Sometimes a professor in this field has all available degrees in child and adolescent development. Other times they have one degree directly in the field. For example, you can have a BA in child psychology or psychology with an MA in child development and a PhD in child and adolescent development. Alternatively, you can have two BA degrees, psychology and education. Then you go on to get a MA in child and adolescent development and then a PhD in educational psychology. The combinations are many, but it usually helps if at least one degree is directly focused in child and adolescent development.

There is certain experience that you need to obtain a position as a child and adolescent development professor (Bok, 2015; Chronicle of Higher Education, 2012), both general and specific according to the position. In general, you need some experience working with children and/or families. You also need some experience teaching at the college level, conducting research, and serving on committees. You typically get these experiences in graduate school. The extent of experience needed varies by institution and level of position. You can be an adjunct professor (lecturer), a tenure-track professor, or a tenured professor. There is a career ladder associated with being a professor: assistant professor, associate professor, and a full professor. Above and beyond these levels and titles, you can become an endowed professor. Additionally, the rungs of the ladder have different qualifications depending on in what college or university setting you work (Bok, 2015). For example, at a two-year community college, teaching skill and student evaluations of your teaching are the most important criteria for retention and promotion in your job. You also have to perform well on various committees at the college and in the local and professional communities. At a four-year research university, you have to publish journal articles of significant intellectual merit and obtain sizable grant money from funding institutions, such as foundations and governmental agencies. You have to do all of this in addition to your teaching responsibilities. Moreover, classes are usually bigger at a four-year university than at a two-year college. The range of class size at a two-year college is usually 15 to 30. At a four-year universities class size runs from 25 students to 500 students in one class. However, usually with 75 or more students, you are provided with an instructional assistant or teaching assistant. Alternatively, if you have a class that has really high enrollment, you may not teach as many classes as your colleagues. All colleges and universities usually have some requirements for teaching, researching, providing service, and leadership that professors at these particular institutions complete. There actually are differences among all colleges and universities, even if they have the same classification or type. There are also differences in student level at various colleges and universities (Bok, 2015; Chronicle of Higher Education, 2012).

Community Colleges

Some colleges and universities focus on undergraduate students and degrees. Moreover, most community colleges offer only two-year Associate (AA) degrees, certificates, and other job training; but this is changing (Meyer, 2012). Students who wish to obtain a Bachelor degree need to transfer to a four-year college or university. So, if you want to teach young, early entry college students and focus the majority of your time teaching, then a community college setting is good for you. However, this setting is not appropriate for everyone and other settings exist. Before we explore other settings, let us read a vignette from a community college professor.

Jesse's Interview

Jesse is a professor in a community college. Her educational background consists of a BA in psychology with a minor in applied developmental psychology and a MA in child development. She is currently working on a PhD in education with an emphasis in learning and mind sciences. She loves her job and cannot see herself doing anything else. She regularly teaches five classes a semester.

She believes her family of origin really impacted her career decision, as her father currently teaches college. Not only that, but her mother and father made education a priority. When she was young her parents took her on college visits and they always discussed education. She knew she would go to college; the only two questions were which college or university and when would she go. She also fell in love with child and adolescent development early in life. She not only attended her aunt's child care center, but when she was an adolescent she also helped her aunt. She really enjoyed helping her aunt and being around children. Her aunt suggested that she major in child and adolescent development.

Jesse has her own family, but she is not sure this has impacted her career choice. She has been married for approximately five years and she recently gave birth. She and her husband had always planned on having children and now those plans are unfolding. It is important to note that Jesse and her husband were high-school homecoming king and queen. They have been together ever since, dating in college and after college, and even beyond that.

Jesse has been a professor for approximately five years. She was a part-time adjunct for one year and has been on the full-time tenure track for four years. To get to this point, she began training adult learners when she was an undergraduate in college. She obtained more experience in grad school training adult learners. After obtaining her MA in child development, she was a site supervisor and coordinator in a child care center for one year. She also was a summer camp coordinator. Then she joined a school district, where she was a program manager for one and a half years and a youth service specialist for two years. Right afterwards, she became a college professor.

As a college professor, Jesse's current title is assistant professor and her days and weeks are flexible. She sees her duties as designing and implementing a high-quality curriculum for adult learners. She designs lectures, visual aids, activities, demonstrations, and assessment materials. She noted that class sizes range from 32 to 60 in a class. She makes sure to deliver course content in a variety of modalities. She tries to build relationships with her students. She also answers questions, grades papers, responds to emails, and responds to phone calls. And then, she says, there are meetings: departmental meetings, college task forces, union meetings, and so on. She is the union liaison and she is trying to encourage more men to enter the field of child and adolescent development. Her last set of duties is building relationships with community organizations. She reads books at local schools and advises organizations in the field of child and adolescent development. On her way to becoming an assistant professor, she has had many turning points and highlights. She gets a lot of joy from her career.

Jesse's first turning point came as an undergraduate. She gave serious thought to what she wanted to do with her career; finally, she decided to follow her passions and not a paycheck. A second turning point also came while she was an undergraduate. One of her professors taught about the achievement gap between lower socioeconomic students and higher socioeconomic students. To this day, the achievement gap really concerns her—to the point that she wants to help narrow it. She is really concerned about the summer downward slide of grades and achievement of lower socioeconomic students. This reminded her of the need for summer programs and helped her realize that she needs a PhD to make the most impact. A third turning point came while she was completing her MA degree. She participated in an internship program at the local community college and really enjoyed it. She discovered she was good at teaching and so she decided to be a professor. So far, her career choice is filled with many joys and just one challenge.

Jesse enjoys the flexibility of her job and building a relationship with her students. She also enjoys both the processes and contents of the teaching and research she is doing. Her biggest joy is feeling like she is making a difference, especially in narrowing the achievement gap. Next, she wants to discover where she can make the biggest impact on narrowing the achievement gap. She wants to utilize her skills and talents to make a difference. This yearning leads to her biggest challenge: she wants to really help and make a big impact, but she is coming to realize that she is only one person and cannot do this all on her own. This realization proves that although she is a young professor, she is quite wise.

This wisdom and other personal characteristics have helped her to succeed in her chosen career. She describes her personal assets in terms of her career as perseverance, intelligence, ambition, a strong work ethic, and appreciation of opportunities and blessings. She also thinks that being sociable and truly enjoying people help her to succeed. Additionally, she takes calculated and planned risks. All of these characteristics help to be a good assistant professor. However, she recognizes that there are outside influences on her career choice and success. Her family of origin and extended family have influenced her greatly. She has also has good relationships with key people in her life that have mentored her, such as professors. The very existence of the achievement gap has influenced her greatly. It has given her a mission and she really wants to have an impact. This mission leads to her advice for someone looking for a career: Follow your passion. Follow what drives and excites you.

Four-Year, Public Universities and Colleges

Four-year colleges and universities offer higher-level degrees than two-year colleges. These colleges and universities offer BA, BS, MA, MS, and MBA, and advanced degrees such as EdS, PhD, EdD, JD, and MD. So the materials and students that you teach will be more advanced. Also, at four-year colleges and universities your duties will probably include more service and research responsibilities. The size of your work setting may also be different depending on where you work. Small colleges may only have around 3,000 students, while large institutions may have upwards of 50,000 to 60,000 students. Four-year colleges and universities may be public or private. Hunter College in New York City and the University of Illinois are examples of four-year public institutions. Harvard and Harvey Mudd are examples of four-year private institutions. Your duties will vary based on the setting. Let us take a look at another interview, this time a new professor at a public four-year university in Arizona. Her name is Susie.

Susie's Interview

Susie has a BA in psychology, a MA in psychology, and a PhD in child and adolescent development. She is an assistant professor with three main duties: research, teaching, and service (minimal). She teaches two classes per semester and spends most of her time on research activities. She has been an assistant professor at a university in Arizona for two years. Before that, she spent three years working as a postdoctoral student on a research project in New York. Susie states that the highlights of her career are obtaining a PhD and getting and completing a postdoc, preparing herself for a career in academia.

Susie really believes that her childhood had an impact on her career choice. She is the youngest of three children and was born in Mexico. She immigrated to the United States at the age of five, learning to speak English in elementary school. She vividly remembers the acculturation process she experienced. (Acculturation is adjusting to a new culture.) As she grew, she became a language interpreter and cultural broker for her parents. All of these experiences influenced her greatly. In high school she became interested in the field of child and adolescent development, especially learning languages, acculturating in a new country, finding your identity, and achieving school success. These topics became an interest and now she studies them as an assistant professor.

Currently, Susie's family consists of her fiancé. They plan on having children, but they are waiting until they have more stability and financial security. Up to this point, Susie has experienced much stress and mobility associated with her chosen career path. Now that she is an assistant professor on the tenure track, life is less stressful.

Her present job consists of research foremost, teaching secondary, and minimal service. She teaches two classes a semester, holds office hours for her students, and writes in the morning. She spends a big part of her time gathering and analyzing data, and writing. She also meets with research collaborators and attends conferences to present her research, hear other research and be current, network, and develop professionally. Additionally, she attends meetings for her department and college.

Susie really enjoys research and teaching, especially seeing the students grow and herself grow as a teacher. Balance is a challenge for her. On some days, she works long hours and sometimes professional work creeps into her personal life. There are days when she works from 6:00 am to 10:00 pm.

Personal characteristics that she has that help her be successful are perseverance and resilience. She can overcome challenges and learn from her experiences. She says it also helps to be understanding and empathetic with students and colleagues.

There have been other, outside influences on her career journey. As the first in her family to obtain a BA, just achieving that degree had a big influence on her. The support she received from faculty along the way was a big influence, too. She wanted to be a professor because of that support and because of the need for women of color in higher education.

Susie's final words are that her parents are immigrants and she was raised in a low socioeconomic status home. However, now she has privilege. She believes in the power of education. She also enjoys supporting her students who come from low socioeconomic status families. These realities help her to really appreciate and have enthusiasm for her job and career.

Private, Nonprofit Colleges and Universities

Private, nonprofit colleges and universities are usually smaller than public colleges and universities, with enrollments of about 2,000 to 20,000. In contrast, public institutions typically have many more students, with a few having around 60,000. Also, the class size is usually smaller at private colleges and universities. Private nonprofit colleges and universities have classes of 25 or 30, while in public institutions class sizes can be up to 300 or 500 students. Although they are nonprofits, private universities usually cost more than public universities (though there are a few exceptions). Private universities still have the same requirements of professors, with a combination of teaching, research, and service. Because of their small size, private universities can be a bit more flexible, with professorial duties that are sometimes blended. Private institutions still have the different types of professors (part-time, full-time, adjunct lecturer) and the different levels for tenure-track professors (assistant, associate, full). The following interview with Arnold illustrates the life of a professor at a private institution.

Arnold's Interview

Arnold has a BA in psychology and a PhD in child and adolescent development. He has been a professor for 22 years and has achieved the rank of full professor. He also performs some administrative duties for his department. He enjoys his job, especially the research aspect. He works hard, sometimes 60 hours per week, and has been persistent throughout his career and life.

When he ponders his early life, he states it did have an impact on him. He and his brother were raised in poverty by a single mother. He was the first in his family to graduate high school, so it goes without saying that he was his first to graduate college and get a PhD. He believes his life story and journey gave him a keen interest in child and adolescent development. He also believes his interest in working with children started early.

Arnold and his wife have two children, who are currently in college themselves. He does not believe that his wife and children have impacted his career choice. However, he did mention it is not always easy to balance work and family.

Arnold's career began at a public university in the South, but currently he is located at a private institution in northern Virginia. In his 22 years, the highlights that mean the most for him are being the editor of one of the renowned journals in his field and traveling internationally for work. He really loves all of his duties, especially research and mentoring students. The challenges have been balancing work and family, and sometimes working 60-hour weeks. However, he loves his job so much that he expects to be working when he is 70 years of age.

When he describes his typical work schedule, he states that he does teaching, research, and service. However, he goes on to focus on the research and service aspects. He currently has an administrative, leadership position in his department that involves lots of meetings. He also mentioned that he writes at home two days a week and currently has 19 papers under review for publication. He really enjoys the varied and flexible schedule and states that research is fun.

The personal characteristics that help him be successful as a full professor are his resilience, organization, motivation, strong work ethic, and persistence. Early experiences working with children and working on research have also influenced him and helped him to thrive on the job. Other external influences are his colleagues.

Leadership Positions in Colleges and Universities

Beginning your career as a professor can lead to leadership positions at the college or university level. For example, Arnold has some administrative and leadership tasks in his present job. Administrative and leadership positions can vary from coordinating a program to being the president or chancellor of a college or university (Bok, 2015). The ladder in higher education leadership can be varied, but usually goes somewhat like this: coordinator, chair, director, assistant dean, associate dean, dean, assistant vice president, associate vice president, vice president, and president. Some professors enter administrative and leadership roles and stay in them. Others lead at the university or college for a time and then return to the ranks of faculty to teaching and other professorial duties. Some professors even obtain degrees in higher education administration and leadership. However, these degrees are not required to become a leader or administrator in a college or university. A professor with degrees in child and adolescent development and related fields can still become the president of a university. Our last interview for this chapter is a professor who also has some low-level administrative responsibilities in his current position in a public institution of higher education. He has some ambition to rise in the ranks of higher education leadership, as well.

Carl's Interview

Carl has a BA in English, an MS in ECE, and a PhD in child and adolescent development. He has more than 22 years of experience as a professor and has currently obtained the rank of associate professor. He plans on becoming a full professor in two or three years and would like to eventually be an higher education dean of his college. Carl has worked in two different universities that were both four-year public institutions. Currently, he is coordinator of ECE programs at a university in Florida, oversees graduate-level certificate program admissions, and oversees curriculum development. He says his main goal in these positions is to maintain high-quality programs that are respected and to ensure students graduate in a timely manner.

Carl believes his early life impacted his career choice. His family was middle class in terms of finances and values. His father was a high schoolteacher and his mother was a librarian—and they both emphasized education. Two of his sisters are elementary schoolteachers.

Carl also states that having his own family has enriched his career. He has one son, who is learning to drive. He said that having his own child gave him more sympathy with parents and those who work with children. He also said that being a parent gives him a better appreciation of what he is teaching and gives him great examples to use in class. Additionally, he said that having his own family changes how he teaches, because he is more patient. It also gives him more practical "street credibility" with his students.

The highlights and turning points in his career have been many. Some of the notable highlights have been getting accepted to graduate school and working with the great scholar Robbie Case. Exposure to Dr. Case and other fantastic scholars has helped him in his life. He has also enjoyed working with the legislature in Florida to improve the quality and stature of ECE. Other highlights have come from advocating for ECE and working with underserved populations. A big turning point was when he changed institutions. He feels that currently he can have a bigger impact where he is and enjoys the fact that he can work with bilingual populations.

Carl teaches three classes per semester as well as coordinating the programs previously mentioned. He also conducts research, which gives him great pleasure. He conducts his research in the community and serves on boards in the community. As part of research, he writes grants and articles, and attends conferences. He also really enjoys serving on doctoral committees. As part of teaching, he evaluates students. He states that it is hard to be perfect in every area of his job, so you prioritize and do the best you can. It also helps if you are efficient.

His main joys in his job are teaching and research, which give him tremendous pleasure, although grading and some parts of research can be tedious. He believes that his work with young children is important and it gives him great pleasure. He is quite content.

In terms of personal characteristics that help him in his job, he immediately says that social skills and an outgoing personality are helpful. He also advises against emphasizing praise or criticism too much, because both are constants in the field and are to be taken with a grain of salt. He says he is also successful at his job because he can separate work and family. In general, he is a supportive and positive person. He is also a good citizen and a hard worker. He likes to set goals and keep improving, hoping one day to be a dean.

Career Specifics

Ethics

As in most professional careers, university professors can join associations that govern their behavior and establish ethical guidelines. The American Association of University Professors (AAUP) is one such organization. The AAUP originally established ethical guidelines for its members and others in the same career in 1966. These guidelines were revised in 2009 and were published again in 2015 (AAUP, 2015). The ethical principles that guide university professors are basically five statements concerning their duties and tasks in relation to their field, their students, their colleagues, their institution, and their community (see Table 7.1). In sum, professors are to;

- Advance knowledge and seek truth.
- Respect students and encourage their learning.
- Never harass or discriminate against colleagues.
- Observe institutional regulations that do not conflict with academic freedom.
- Promote free inquiry and further public understanding of academic freedom.

Salary

Salaries for university professionals vary depending on the type of institution, the field, the state in which you work, and your rank. For instance, the average salary for an assistant professor in a two-year university is $54,162 and in a four-year university it is $63,441, while a full professor at a four-year university has an average salary of $103,947 (see

Table 7.1 Ethics for Professors

The Statement

1. Professors, guided by a deep conviction of the worth and dignity of the advancement of knowledge, recognize the special responsibilities placed upon them. Their primary responsibility to their subject is to seek and to state the truth as they see it. To this end professors devote their energies to developing and improving their scholarly competence. They accept the obligation to exercise critical self-discipline and judgment in using, extending, and transmitting knowledge. They practice intellectual honesty. Although professors may follow subsidiary interests, these interests must never seriously hamper or compromise their freedom of inquiry.

2. As teachers, professors encourage the free pursuit of learning in their students. They hold before them the best scholarly and ethical standards of their discipline. Professors demonstrate respect for students as individuals and adhere to their proper roles as intellectual guides and counselors. Professors make every reasonable effort to foster honest academic conduct and to ensure that their evaluations of students reflect each student's true merit. They respect the confidential nature of the relationship between professor and student. They avoid any exploitation, harassment, or discriminatory treatment of students. They acknowledge significant academic or scholarly assistance from them. They protect their academic freedom.

3. As colleagues, professors have obligations that derive from common membership in the community of scholars. Professors do not discriminate against or harass colleagues. They respect and defend the free inquiry of associates, even when it leads to findings and conclusions that differ from their own. Professors acknowledge academic debt and strive to be objective in their professional judgment of colleagues. Professors accept their share of faculty responsibilities for the governance of their institution.

4. As members of an academic institution, professors seek above all to be effective teachers and scholars. Although professors observe the stated regulations of the institution, provided the regulations do not contravene academic freedom, they maintain their right to criticize and seek revision. Professors give due regard to their paramount responsibilities within their institution in determining the amount and character of work done outside it. When considering the interruption or termination of their service, professors recognize the effect of their decision upon the program of the institution and give due notice of their intentions.

5. As members of their community, professors have the rights and obligations of other citizens. Professors measure the urgency of these obligations in the light of their responsibilities to their subject, to their students, to their profession, and to their institution. When they speak or act as private persons, they avoid creating the impression of speaking or acting for their college or university. As citizens engaged in a profession that depends upon freedom for its health and integrity, professors have a particular obligation to promote conditions of free inquiry and to further public understanding of academic freedom.

Source: American Association of University Professors (2015). Reprinted with permission of Johns Hopkins University Press.

Table 7.2). As another example, a child and adolescent development professor in an education field or college in Arizona averages $65,710. That same professor in a psychology field or department in Ohio makes an average of $79,610, as can be seen in Table 7.3.

Also mentioned in this chapter was the prospect of moving up into an administrative position at a college or university. Of course, salary then increases. The amount of increase varies by the administrative position held and the type of higher education institution. Please consult the Bureau of Labor Statistics or the Chronicle of Higher Education if you are interested in salary details for higher education administrators.

Table 7.2 Average Salaries by Rank

	Professor	Associate Professor	Assistant Professor	Adjunct Lecturer
Public				
Four-year	$103,947	$75,250	$63,441	$50,047
Men	$107,192	$77,281	$65,534	$52,163
Women	$95,045	$72,297	$61,165	$48,453
Two-year	$72,377	$60,633	$54,162	$58,431
Men	$74,425	$61,565	$54,913	$59,108
Women	$70,429	$59,853	$53,582	$57,835

Source: Chronicle of Higher Education (2012)

Table 7.3 Salaries by Department and State

State	General Postsecondary Department	Annual Mean Salary
Arizona	Engineering	$100,940
Arizona	Psychology	$72,860
Arizona	Education	$65,710
California	Engineering	$114,760
California	Psychology	$86,890
California	Education	$72,290
Ohio	Engineering	$95,840
Ohio	Psychology	$79,610
Ohio	Education	$61,600

Source: Chronicle of Higher Education (2012)

Summary

Higher education professor and administrator positions are varied, flexible, and found in many different settings. In regards to child and adolescent development as a career, you can work in a college of education or a psychology department. You can also work in varied college or university settings, including two-year colleges and four-year colleges and universities; these institutions can be either public or private. The settings have some differences and similarities. All professors have the duties of teaching, research, and providing service, but the emphasis on these three duties vary. You can work part-time as an adjunct lecturer or full-time on the tenure track. On the tenure track there are three levels: assistant professor, associate professor, and full professor.

Reflective Questions

1. Should higher education, at least the first two years, be compulsory for everyone? Is college the correct path for everyone?
2. Should a college education be free to all who aspire to achieve it? Will the tax dollars invested produce a good return on its investment?

3. Should college professors have to get a teaching credential as K–12 teachers do?
4. Are academic freedom and tenure good for the quality of higher education?

Is This Right for You?

Do you get excited by constantly learning and improving and proving yourself? Do you also love nurturing others who may benefit from your interactions and advice? Do you like juggling multiple roles and responsibilities? If you answered "yes" to those questions, you may want to consider being a college professor.

This profession offers a variety of job responsibilities and opportunities. Usually, professors teach, conduct research, and provide service in some combination. There are also the various levels mentioned previously. You can work part-time or full-time. You can be an adjunct professor, lecturer, visiting professor, or tenure-track professor. Once you obtain tenure, you can move up the ladder to higher levels. The route you can take starts as an assistant professor, and goes to an associate professor, and then a full professor. If you want to continue into administration, there are also options. These options include department chair, program coordinator, program director, college dean, vice president, provost, president, and other positions. There are many options and various pathways, but this profession may not be for everyone.

This profession requires extended education completion. Not everyone wants to complete the MA or MS degree that is required to enter the profession. Then there is the completion of a doctoral degree and a culminating dissertation in order to advance at a four-year college. Sometimes there is even a pay differential at two-year community colleges between the MA or MS degree-holder and a doctoral degree-holder. Consider the fact that the doctoral degree may be needed for an entry level position in the future, so you really need to love education to choose this career. You also have to know how to balance several differing duties, manage your time and schedule, and prioritize competing demands. Remember that some weeks require 60 hours of work, but the work is quite fulfilling and satisfying. If you are still excited and motivated to enter the higher education arena of child and adolescent development, then this is the career for you.

References

American Association of University Professor (2015). Statement of professional ethics. In *Policy documents and reports* (11th ed., pp. 91–93). Baltimore, MD: Johns Hopkins University Press.

Bok, D. C. (2015). *Higher education in America*. Princeton, NJ: Princeton University Press.

Chronicle of Higher Education (2012). Chronicle of higher education. *The profession: Almanac issue*, 58(1), 22–29.

Meyer, L. H. (2012). Negotiating academic values, professorial responsibilities and expectations for accountability in today's university. *Higher Education Quarterly*, 66(2), 207–217.

Chapter 8

Nonprofit Organizations

Nonprofit organizations offer educators within the field of child and adolescent development a unique opportunity to develop, improve, and provide important services for the healthy development of children and families. According to the Legal Information Institute at Cornell Law School (n.d.), nonprofit organizations can be charitable, educational, religious, scientific, or focused on literary activities. Therefore, they can include a range of institutions such as universities, churches, hospitals, museums, legal aid societies, professional associations, and public charities, among other entities. Money to support nonprofit organizations is often generated through government contracts and grants, foundations, corporate philanthropy, fundraising, charitable contributions from individuals, and the sale of products. However, the income that is generated is not distributed to its members and administrators; instead, the money goes toward the operations of the organization in providing important services to the public. Nonprofit organizations typically follow their state-recommended guidelines for effective practices in governance and operation, fiscal management, and in ensuring that the mission of the organization is upheld in all its activities. Nonprofit organizations are great places to work for educators who are self-directed, creative, and are comfortable exploring multiple solutions to a problem. The current chapter will discuss some common job positions within nonprofit organizations, explore the mission of well-established nonprofits, and outline the essential skills needed to pursue careers in nonprofit organizations that focus on children and families.

Nonprofit Positions and Careers

Careers within the nonprofit sector range from voluntary and entry-level positions to leadership roles, with many nonprofits preferring individuals with a liberal arts education (or a broad education), given the many tasks in which employees are often engaged. However, it is imperative for educators to carefully review the job descriptions of various positions for preferred qualifications and education, so as to understand the degrees and certifications needed for desired positions. Important position descriptions and duties are discussed below.

Volunteers

Nonprofit organizations often recruit volunteers to assist with short- and long-term projects, as well as with major events. Volunteering is a great way for students, recent graduates, and prospective employees to learn about an organization, its inner workings, and the people who work there, as well as to gain a better sense of different job positions within the organization. It is wise to seek volunteer positions that speak to your interests and skills, such as conducting research, writing grants, and organizing and managing events, etc.

Committee Members

Committees are very important to nonprofit organizations, as they help steer an organization's employees in particular areas. Volunteers could join the budget or finance committee, where they oversee the development of the budget, monitor funds, and review major grants. Joining the public relations committee would allow members to bring community awareness to the organization by communicating with the press. Additional committees of interest might include board development, evaluation, fundraising, promotion and sales, personnel, and marketing, as well as ad hoc committees such as the ethics committee, which monitors the ethical behavior of all employees, the research committee, which gathers data for program improvements, and the events committee, which is dedicated to increasing fundraising activities.

Board of Directors

The board of directors ensures that the nonprofit organization is pursuing its mission, is financially stable, and meets all legal obligations. There is a chairperson who runs board meetings, a vice chair who acts as chair when s/he is not present, a treasurer who overseas the financial responsibilities of the organization, and an administrative assistant who takes notes. Additional board members attend all meetings, vote on official matters, and serve on various committees.

Executive Director or CEO

The executive director or CEO is the business manager for a nonprofit organization, is knowledgeable about its rules and regulations, and reports to the board of directors.

Development Staff

Development staff are engaged in activities such as fundraising, political lobbying, public awareness campaigns, donor management, and event planning. The development director manages staff, works with the executive director and finance department, and engages in marketing duties.

Advisory Board

The advisory board is made up of groups of experts who guide the organization in specific areas. Advisory board members might include academic scholars, community leaders, and other key individuals depending on the subject in which advice is needed.

Please note that there are many positions available within any nonprofit organization, including research analysts, field educators, and program managers, to name a few, that help to further the mission of the organization. As previously mentioned, educators should seek positions at nonprofit organizations that speak to their unique interests and skills.

Familiar Nonprofit Organizations

Some well-established nonprofit organizations include the American Heart Association, March of Dimes, Children's Defense Fund, and Make-A-Wish Foundation. These organizations have been highly publicized for their humanitarian work in improving the lives of children, adults, and families. They are a great place to start in exploring the various types of careers that exist within the nonprofit sector. However, it is recommended that educators not only explore careers within well-established and large nonprofit organizations, like those mentioned here, but to also explore smaller nonprofits that are in need of assistance in establishing their reach and impact on local communities. Keep in mind that some nonprofit organizations have a global or national reach, while other organizations have a state focused or local community reach. By exploring nonprofit organizations that speak to specific interests, educators will be able to engage in meaningful work that will enhance their lives and the lives of others.

American Heart Association

The American Heart Association (www.heart.org) was founded in 1924 by six cardiologists and is now the nation's oldest and largest voluntary organization that focuses on strengthening public health policies, while also providing tools and information on saving and improving lives. The American Stroke Association (www.strokeassociation.org) was created as a division of the American Heart Association and is focused on stroke-related activities. The American Heart Association provides health education, CPR education, and research-based guidelines for patient treatment and healthy lifestyle choices, along with vital information for policy makers and advocates on protecting and improving the health of all communities. Both organizations receive continued support from physicians, scientists, and volunteers, and they have created a national network for research, education, community programming, fundraising, and advocacy on heart disease and stroke. Volunteer and professional positions range from advocacy to fundraising.

March of Dimes

The March of Dimes (www.marchofdimes.org) was founded by President Franklin D. Roosevelt in 1938 to address the polio epidemic, as the disease had left him with a physical disability. The foundation funded research for vaccines and established a patient aid program to end the polio epidemic in the United States. Once its mission was complete, the foundation turned its focus to the prevention of birth defects and infant mortality through funding research, promoting newborn screenings, providing education on healthy pregnancies and infant care, and developing campaigns such as a multi-year prematurity campaign to increase awareness of premature births. Internships are available for college students and recent graduates, with internships in Washington DC, for those individuals seeking a career in advocacy work at the state and federal levels. Advocacy activities might include advancing maternal and child health policies (e.g., access to quality healthcare), as well as endorsing medical and scientific research that will aid in the organization's health education and prevention efforts. Professional positions are also available within the organization.

Children's Defense Fund

The Children's Defense Fund (www.childrensdefense.org) is a national nonprofit organization that was founded in 1973 to ensure the healthy development of all children by supporting policies and programs that protect children from the consequences of poverty, abuse, and neglect. The organization supports programs that promote quality health care, education, and a strong moral and spiritual foundation for children. Thus, the organization's overall mission is to "ensure every child a *healthy start*, a *head start*, a *fair start*, a *safe start*, and a *moral start* in life, [as well as] successful passage to adulthood with the help of caring families and communities" (Children's Defense Fund, n.d.). Support is received through foundation and cooperate grants, individual donations, and advocates nationwide. The organization is able to help children at the national, state, and community levels, where cross-cultural and interfaith discussions, intergenerational mentoring, and spiritual renewal are emphasized. Internships are available for undergraduate and graduate students, as well as recent graduates, who have a desire to engage in child advocacy and public policy work. Professional positions are also available within the organization.

Make-A-Wish

The Make-A-Wish Foundation (www.worldwish.org) was founded in 1980 and has committed itself to granting wishes to children suffering from life-threatening medical conditions (progressive, degenerative, or malignant illnesses). Granting wishes helps children to feel a sense of hope, strength, and joy. Volunteers, donors, sponsors, medical professionals, and community advocates work hard to ensure that every eligible child receives his or her wish (e.g., to be a police officer, superhero, ballerina, car designer, etc.), which often inspires children to continue fighting against their illnesses and to comply with medical treatments, as well as improving their emotional health. The values of the foundation include integrity (honesty, transparency, and respect), a focus on the child ("wish children"), excellence (in practice), community (including collaborative efforts among staff, volunteers, donors, and the global community), and inspiration (derived from life-affirming enthusiasm, imagination, and creativity). The foundation has chapters across the nation with professional positions and internships available, ranging from operational support to information technology, such as internet communication.

Desired Knowledge, Skills, and Abilities

There are many skills that educators will need in order to effectively function within the nonprofit sector and in improving the lives of children and families. Following are descriptions of key competencies, skills, and abilities.

Cultural Competence

Nonprofit organizations that focus on children and families will likely have a social justice focus that underscores the need for employees to understand diverse cultural norms, values, and beliefs systems. This type of knowledge can aid team members in understanding diverse communities, so as to develop unique solutions and culturally appropriate practices, services, and programming. The National Council of Nonprofits (2017) endorses diversity, inclusion, and equity as core values that should drive the mission, goals, and activities of any nonprofit organization. Therefore, many nonprofits seek to hire individuals with diverse viewpoints and skills, as innovation comes from examining a problem through many different lenses. Educators should increase their cultural competency through research and interacting with children and families from diverse communities.

Self-Starter (Self-Directed)

The ability to understand a goal and to reach that goal with little to no direction, or in collaboration with others, is a sought-after skill in an industry where roles are not always defined. Therefore, educators should develop the ability to problem-solve and execute plans, with little direction, in order to become a valuable member of any organization.

Data Savvy

The ability to collect, analyze, display, and disseminate data efficiently and effectively is extremely important. Many nonprofits are data driven in order to evaluate their effectiveness, reach, and social impact. Therefore, educators who can comfortably work with data and produce infographics (e.g., charts, diagrams, and figures) will be highly sought after in the nonprofit sector.

Design Thinking

Design thinking is also known as *solution-based thinking,* and provides an important method for addressing complicated social issues related to poverty, education reform, immigration reform, and the like. In the field of child and adolescent development, *scientific thinking* is emphasized, where research questions, hypotheses, theoretical frameworks, and data are utilized to develop objective policy recommendations. Design thinking explores many creative solutions by incorporating emotional content, such as consumer feedback. Brown (2009) discusses how design thinking moves through four mental stages: *divergent thinking* (generating many solutions to a problem), *convergent thinking* (deciding on the most realistic solution), *analysis* (exploring patterns), and *synthesis* (identifying meaningful patterns). Evaluating the execution and impact of ideas is important, so as to improve solutions. Thus, experimentation is key with design thinking: individuals must be flexible in their thinking and open to exploring ideas that excite them and their teammates. Educators should utilize scientific thinking to inform aspects of design thinking, in order to cultivate high-level thinking skills that will be valuable on the job.

Collaborative Spirit

Knowing how to work collaboratively within your department, across departments, and with community members and other organizations is important. While individuals will be tasked with numerous assignments, these assignments will rarely, if ever, be completed without feedback. Individuals usually work in a team setting, where team members work on aspects of a problem both alone and in partnership with one another. Educators who enjoy working alone will need to develop the ability to effectively and consistently collaborate with colleagues.

Strong Work Ethic and Ability to Work Long Hours

A strong work ethic is important at any nonprofit organization, as the issues being addressed impact the lives of many. Overcoming challenges, taking on multiple roles, and working beyond the typical 9–5 work day (including evenings and weekends) are typical when working for a nonprofit. Therefore, educators must be equipped with the dedication and endurance to work long and challenging hours to help their organizations to reach its goals.

Innovation

Creativity is extremely important in addressing complex issues, so as to reach an organization's goals. It is important to understand that there are many ways to address a problem and being able to think outside the box is necessary. Educators must tap into their education-based knowledge, diverse experiences, and creative spirit to work with colleagues in addressing important issues.

Time Management Skills

Accomplishing tasks in a timely manner is a valuable skill, as all team members and collaborative entities rely on each other to meet overall goals and deadlines. Therefore, educators must know how to produce meaningful work in a timely manner that is consistent with the culture of the organization.

Adaptability

Adapting to the culture of your organization, both socially and in regard to skill development, takes emotional competence and the ability to translate your current skills to the job at hand. As an educator, you must strive to adapt to new environments in order to function effectively.

On a final note, it is okay not to know everything about an issue, an organization, or to have all the skills listed in this chapter. However, you should be willing to research issues, develop a deeper understanding of your organization's mission, and dedicate yourself to developing the skills necessary to become successful within your organization—motivation and a can-do attitude are key.

Recommended Practices

State associations have guidelines and ethical practices for the effective functioning of nonprofit organizations that range from financial transparency to demonstrating outcomes and effectiveness. Following are some recommended practices for nonprofit board members in three states, as they relate to financial management, governance and operations, and the mission of the nonprofit. Please keep in mind that Tables 8.1–8.3 focus only on a few state-recommended practices.

Table 8.1 Indiana ~ Best Practices Checklist

Financial Management	"The nonprofit has a good financial plan that provides for financial resources that support the programs and services consistent with the nonprofit's mission."
Governance and Operations	"The governing board formulates budgetary priorities, adopts an annual budget prior to the start of the fiscal year and adopts a funding plan for securing resources to implement the nonprofit's annual goals and objectives."
Nonprofit Mission	"The nonprofit has a clear and coherent written plan for the future, i.e. 3–10 year strategic plan with well defined, measurable and achievable goals and action steps with timeframes."

Source: Indiana Attorney General (n.d.)

Table 8.2 Ohio ~ Charitable Organization Guidelines

Financial Management	"Board members are to develop annual budgets that provide clear direction for all organizational spending. The budget should be a blueprint of the board's program plans and should be routinely monitored, tracked throughout the year, and revised as necessary."
Governance and Operations	"Be familiar with state and federal laws relating to nonprofit entities, fundraising, and tax-related issues as well as legal issues connected with the organization's charitable purposes and operations."
Nonprofit Mission	"Oversee the executive director and ensure that the charity's purposes are fulfilled efficiently and follow sound business standards"

Source: Ohio Attorney General (n.d.)

Table 8.3 Washington~ Best Practices

Financial Management	"Direct and indirect costs are monitored, including allocation of staff time to program, administration, evaluation, and fundraising activities."
Governance and operations	"Development of plan includes organization strengths, weaknesses, opportunities and challenges on a continuous basis and incorporates those observations into the strategic plan."
Nonprofit Mission	"Board sets and monitors policies and attends to emerging policy issues."

Source: Whatcom Council of Nonprofits (n.d.)

Interview With Aisha Lowe, PhD

Dr. Aletha M. Harven, one of the book's authors, conducted a brief interview with her good friend and colleague, Dr. Aisha Lowe, who is currently Associate Dean of the Office of Academic Research and Associate Professor in the School of Education at a university in California. She has her Bachelor of Arts degree in Psychology with an emphasis in Child Development, a Master of Arts degree in Sociology, and a PhD in Education Psychology with an emphasis in Child Development. Prior to her current position, Dr. Lowe worked for three nonprofit organizations. Given that both Dr. Harven and Dr. Lowe have worked in the nonprofit sector, Dr. Harven wanted to interview Dr. Lowe to learn more about her unique experiences. Following is a summary of their interview, as documented by Dr. Harven.

Why a Nonprofit?

When I asked Dr. Lowe what inspired her to work in the nonprofit sector for several years, she informed me that she was looking to make a difference in the lives of low-income students. She said that her interest in outreach work began when she was in high school, assisting with an upward bound program for low-income middle school students that prepared them for high school. Dr. Lowe's desire to help underserved children lead to her taking on various jobs that had both a direct and indirect impact on diverse youth. Her direct impact came from her work in a tutoring and sports program on a university campus, while her indirect impact came from her work in research, policy, and advocacy.

Nonprofit Work

When I asked Dr. Lowe to tell me about her nonprofit job positions, she informed me about her position as a tutorial director on a university campus, where she worked for two years. At the time, she had her Bachelor of Arts degree. The tutoring program trained undergraduate students to work one-on-one with underserved high school students to increase their academic engagement and achievement. The program also sought to increase children's involvement in enrichment and sports activities. Dr. Lowe oversaw student tutors, as well as tutors from the local community. After graduating with her PhD and working as a schoolteacher, Dr. Lowe worked as a data analyst for two years at a state charter school association, which was a nonprofit organization that was financially supported by charter schools in return for support, lobbying, and political advocacy. Dr. Lowe went on to become the organization's director of research for two additional years. Her work had an indirect impact on children, as policy recommendations were based on the research she and her team generated. It is noteworthy that most of her time was spent in an office rather than on the ground with students, teachers, and caregivers. Next, Dr. Lowe became an executive director for a nonprofit advocacy and public policy organization that focused on school reform and school choice efforts in her local community. Support for the organization was sought among African American leaders, churches, and community members. Dr. Lowe stated that her interest in the organization came from a desire to engage in grassroots reform work, which placed her in direct contact with the community she wanted to impact. After two years at the organization, Dr. Lowe returned to academia, but she continues to engage in outreach work.

Beneficial Skills

When I asked Dr. Lowe to discuss the skills she thought were important for educators to cultivate for a successful transition to the nonprofit sector, she emphasized the importance of being motivated, a self-starter, and having the ability to understand an organization's goals, so as to confidently engage in tasks that help accomplish those goals. She mentioned how educators should be comfortable with working alone and in collaboration, both within and across departments, as work is often done in relation to larger organizational goals. Other important skills that she emphasized included the ability to bring people together around a common goal, being innovative, and being able to effectively problem solve. Dr. Lowe discussed how working hard—often beyond regular hours and into the evenings and on weekends—was common, especially when organizing and attending community events. Dr. Lowe further stated that a flexible schedule and dedication to the mission of an organization was important, so the additional work hours do not "feel like a painful sacrifice."

Career Specifics

Salary

Table 8.4 Salary Table

Select Positions	Average Salaries
Executive Director / CEO	$60,000–$132,000
Director of Development	$48,000–$98,000
Marketing Coordinator	$36,000–$47,000
Communications Manager	$49,000–$69,000
Chief Financial Officer	$48,000–$102,000
Program Manager	$47,000–$52,000
Special Events Manager	$45,000–$53,000
Program Coordinator	$24,000–$38,000
Administrative Assistant	$15–$21/hr

Note: Salaries found on Glassdoor (https://www.glassdoor.com/salaries)

Summary

Given all that has been discussed thus far, educators should consider work in the nonprofit world so as to take advantage of unique opportunities to develop, improve, and provide important services to children and families in need.

Reflective Questions

1. How do you feel about endorsing a social justice agenda when addressing issues that impact the lives of diverse children, caregivers, and families?
2. How might you use your degrees and talents to help children, caregivers, and families in a nonprofit organization that serves them?
3. Which of the skills discussed in this chapter do you currently possess? Which skills will you need to cultivate in order to find success in the nonprofit sector?

Is This Right for You?

1. In what ways will working for a nonprofit organization impact your life?
2. Which nonprofit agencies speak to your interests and desired career goals?
3. What degree(s) will you need to reach your desired career goals within the nonprofit sector?

References

American Heart Association (n.d.). Retrieved from https://healthyforgood.heart.org

Brown, T. (2009). *Change by design: How design thinking transforms organizations and inspires innovation.* New York: HarperCollins.

Children's Defense Fund (n.d.). Retrieved from www.childrensdefense.org

Cornell Law School Legal Information Institute (n.d.). *Nonprofit organizations.* Retrieved from www.law.cornell.edu/wex/nonprofit_organizations

Indiana Attorney General (n.d.). *Best practices checklist for nonprofits*. Retrieved from www.in.gov/attorneygeneral/files/checklist_cover_your_assets_8_29.pdf

Make A Wish (n.d.). Retrieved from http://wish.org/

March of Dimes (n.d.). Retrieved from www.marchofdimes.org/

National Council of Nonprofits (2017). *Why diversity, inclusion, and equity matter for nonprofits*. Retrieved from www.councilofnonprofits.org/tools-resources/why-diversity-inclusion-and-equity-matter-nonprofits

Ohio Attorney General (n.d.). *Guide for charity board members*. Retrieved from www.ohioattorney-general.gov/Files/Publications-Files/Publications-for-Non-Profits/GuideforCharityBoardMembers

Whatcom Council of Nonprofits (n.d.). *Best practices for executive directors and board of nonprofit organizations*. Retrieved from www.floridaliteracy.org/toolkitfiles/BestPractices.pdf

Chapter 9

Counseling and School Psychology

In this chapter we will discuss positions in counseling and school psychology. These positions are obtainable with a BA in child and adolescent development as a foundation, but completing additional education is needed. In other words, you have to continue your education beyond the BA to a MA, and EdS (Educational Specialist), a PhD or other doctorate. Additionally, you will need a license in some states, such as California. Within the field of counseling, there are different types of counselors. In this chapter we will discuss school counselors; marriage, family, and child counselors (MFCCs) and marriage and family therapists (MFT); and career counselors. This chapter will also discuss school psychologists, who play a different role and have different training than school counselors. School psychologists usually assess children's developmental levels, behavioral functioning, and abilities with psychological tests. School counselors interact with children more on a daily basis and perform a different set of duties.

Career Counselors

Description and Preparation

Career counselors help people to find work that they find to be satisfying at all points along their career path (Gordon, 2006). Career counselors help college and university students find work in alignment with their degree and interests. However, career counselors also help mid-career people who are changing career direction or who may be burnt out in their career. They can also aid people toward the end of their career transition into retirement. More and more career counselors are expected to provide emotional and social support and to be culturally competent, much as a MFCC or school counselor (Vespia, Fitzpatrick, Fouad, Kantamneni, & Chen, 2010). Becoming a career counselor requires at least a MA in the field and some positions may require doctorate, either a PhD, a Psy D, or a EdD. A BA in child and adolescent development is a good starting place.

Duties and Workplace Settings

Duties include assessing various career aspects of a client, helping clients create products related to obtaining a job, communicating with clients (written and oral forms), and sometimes making formal presentations (giving talks or teaching). Career counselors assess personality, characteristics, abilities, skills, interests, and values of their clients using standardized and normed tests. Some of these tests are mentioned in Chapter 13. They also help clients create résumés and cover letters, help them search for jobs, and help them secure and prepare for interviews. They can also make speeches and teach mini-lessons to small groups. The amount of these duties that are performed depend on the settings in which the career counselor works.

Most career counselors work in a college or university settings. Some work for a private employer or in a career consulting business. Still others work for government agencies or nonprofit entities. A few may be employed in a high school or secondary school setting.

Marriage, Family, and Child Counselors

Description and Training

MFCCs are sometimes called MFTs, and they are similar in training. Although a BA in child and adolescent development is a good foundation, to practice a MA, MS, or MEd is required. In most states, you also have to obtain a license by passing an exam and spending some time supervised by a licensed practitioner to prove core competency (Miller, Todahl, & Platt, 2010). Some MFCCs have doctoral degrees and conduct research as well as assist clients (Karam & Sprenkle, 2010; Wampler, 2010). In general, MFCCs and MFTs support their clients emotionally and socially. They help their clients to cope with stressors, resolve conflicts, and communicate in marital or parenting relationships. However, they cannot prescribe medicine, because only psychiatrists with MD degrees can perform that duty.

Duties and Settings

MFTs and MFCCs spend their time counseling clients individually or in small groups. They also keep notes and reports about counseling sessions (which usually last 45–60 minutes). Sometimes, depending on their work setting, they also teach classes to small groups on issues surrounding mental health. They can work in private practice, hospitals, religious institutions, governmental agencies, and nonprofit agencies.

School Counselors

General Description, Training, Duties, and Settings

School counselors help children from transitional kindergarten to 12th grade in a variety of ways (Collins, 2014; Dixon, Tucker, & Clark, 2010; Young & Kaffenberger, 2015). They may help older children choose courses and get into college. They may also provide social and emotional support, helping with coping skills, conflict resolution, anger management, and effective communication. Sometimes they help students transition from one grade level to the next. Sometimes they teach small classes to students on mental health issues related to schools, such as bullying and peer mediation. Some school counselors advocate for their students' needs. Training needed to become a school counselor includes at least a MA, MS, or MEd degree and some time spent with practicing with a professional supervisor (DeKruif & Pehrsson, 2011; Swank & Tyson, 2012). Let us look at a personal account of school counseling.

Kerrie's Interview

Kerrie lives and works in Vermont. She has a BA in psychology, a MA in general psychology, and a MS in school counseling. This is Kerrie's educational path, but you can also become a school counselor with a BA in child and adolescent development and a graduate degree in school counseling. Kerrie has been a school counselor for seven years now. For two of those years she worked part-time and for five of those years, full-time. She is married and has two children.

Kerrie believes that her early family life and her current family had an impact on her career choice. She loved playing with her younger cousins and spending time with younger children when she was a teenager. She attended a Catholic elementary school. Her transition to a public middle school was a challenge, because she experienced relational aggression and bullying. However, she had a supportive counselor to aid in this transition and she also participated in sports. When Kerrie was in high school, she provided peer support to fellow students and assisted the high school counselor. She also volunteered to help first and second graders read. All of these experiences demonstrated her love for counseling and supporting others. She thought she wanted to be a school psychologist until she discovered that they conduct testing; she then became interested in school counseling, partly because she wanted flexible hours and summer vacations. She wanted to have children some day and wanted to have a schedule similar to her children's.

Katie considers all steps along her career journey to be key points and highlights. She started out as a learning specialist in a high school in Vermont, which reminded her of her own high school years providing peer support. She then went to graduate school, where she served as a counselor intern in the local schools. She decided that she ultimately wanted to be an elementary school counselor, because she could make a big impact during important years of a child's life. She also enjoyed working in schools, where she could actually teach lessons and be proactive.

As a school counselor, her days are all different, as are all phases of the year. Some of her tasks are teaching short lessons on topics such as bullying, healthy eating, problem solving, relationships and communicating, mindfulness, and yoga. She also meets with parents, writes IEPs, coordinates a Students with Disabilities class, makes phone calls, meets with teachers, meets with the school nurse, and meets with the principal. Her days are full and there is no typical pattern. This is how she likes it.

She has two main challenges: she works in an isolated rural environment, and she has to manage parent expectations. In addition, not everyone really understands the role of school counselors. Sometimes she has to explain her role to nurses, teachers, other school personnel, and parents. Her joys are her job and being with the children. She really likes her job with its flexibility and variety. She thinks that her role as a school counselor is a very important one.

The characteristics she has that help her in her current position are that she is open and flexible, taking situations as they come. She is also organized and a hard worker. Most importantly, she is kind and a good listener.

School Psychologists

Description and Preparation

School psychologists usually have an advanced degree. They may have an EdS (Educational Specialist) or some type of doctorate, usually a PhD or PsyD. However, a BA in child and adolescent development is a good foundation. School psychologists assess children in the school setting who may have special needs or disabilities. They also write IEPs for children who have special needs or disabilities. More and more school psychologists are asked to provide actual therapy or counseling to children in a school setting to support social and emotional needs (Fenning, Diaz, Valley-Gray, Cash, Spearman, Hazel, . . . &

Harris, 2015; Hanchon & Fernald, 2013). In addition, as schools in the United States become more diverse, school psychologists are being asked to help schools work with that diversity (Garcia-Joslin, Carrillo, Guzman, Vega, Plotts, & Lasser, 2016). Since school psychologists have specialized training, they may be asked to supervise school counselors or other personnel (Eagle, Dowd-Eagle, Snyder, & Holtzman, 2015). They may also be asked to help make school decisions at the administrative level. In other words, they may be asked to help develop school policy (Eagle, Dowd-Eagle, Snyder, & Holtzman, 2015).

Daily Duties and Work Settings

School psychologists usually work in public or private schools, but they may work in a school district office. Additionally, they may also work in private practice and see clients and their families on an individual basis. School psychologists spend most of their day assessing children's abilities, developmental levels, and behaviors with standardized tests. They write reports about their findings, which they communicate to school administrators, schoolteachers, parents, families, and others as needed. Sometimes they provide social and emotional support to students in small groups or in individual counseling sessions. They may also supervise other psychologists and counselors. In addition, they assist in school administration and policy making when appropriate. Now, let us look at the career experience of a real school psychologist.

Sam's Interview

Sam is a practicing school psychologist and a professor of school psychology. He has a BS in psychology with an emphasis in child development and a MS in school psychology with a credential in school psychology. He also has a PhD in education with an emphasis in psychological studies. He has had quite a long career: he was a school psychologist for 12 years, then a lead school psychologist for six years. He has been university professor and in private practice for 16 years.

Sam believes that his early years influenced his career choice. His mother taught first grade and his father was an elementary school principal, so every day of his life was focused on school. His parents would have discussions about school from their own perspectives, with his mother speaking from the classroom view and his father from the lead administrative view.

He also believes that being a parent has influenced his career because it has given him genuine empathy; he is able to see through the parents' eyes.

Sam has vivid memories of three specific turning points in his career journey. In his first year as a school psychologist he learned to prioritize, to be organized, and to delegate some of his tasks and responsibilities. His third year was also quite memorable: during that year, a fifth grader shot a sixth grader in the head. The principal looked to Sam for guidance, and he had to design and enact a plan to support the whole school, including students, staff, and families. A third milestone in his career is more recent: he is now trying to understand how to support students, families, and schools when all are experiencing chronic and acute traumatic stressors. Understanding and helping others is really important to Sam.

Sam's career has given him many joyous moments and some challenging ones, too. The challenging moments have included identifying disabilities and communicating those to parents and families. Some other challenges include delivering other difficult news, such as IEP information, health issues, discipline issues, and on some occasions death. He also said that there does not seem to be enough hours in the day. The main joy of being a school psychologist has been working with children. He enjoys helping children with learning disabilities and challenges to overcome. Working with the children makes everything worth it. He is also very appreciative of the fact that no two days are alike: he likes having days that are unpredictable. Some of the tasks related to Sam's job as a school psychologist include assessing children's development and cognitive processing, communicating with families, writing reports, working with teachers and parents to support students, and advocating on behalf of his private clients and their families.

The skills needed to be a good school psychologist are many. Sam believes he is good at his job because he enjoys interacting with children at all ages and phases along development. He also has good interpersonal skills. He has honed this particular skill over time, because school psychologists need to have difficult conversations and solve challenging problems. He says he also is a good listener and a good writer. School psychologists have to be good writers, according to Sam, because they write many reports and documents.

Career Specifics

Ethics

As with all professions, counselors must abide by ethical principles and guidelines. There are several professional organizations that provide guidelines for the professions discussed in this chapter. The American Counseling Association (ACA) provides guidelines for all counselors, both career and school counselors. The American Association of Marriage and Family Therapists provide guidance for MFTs. School psychologists are governed by two major organizations: the American Psychological Association and the National Association of School Psychologists. The National Association of School Psychologists' Ethical Principles will be provided in this textbook, since they are more targeted and specific for this particular profession.

American Counseling Association

The ACA provides a comprehensive description of ethical behavior for its members that includes a mission, an ethical preamble, and an ethical purpose. These three sections are followed by detailed ethical standards presented in nine categories.

The ACA's mission speaks of enhancing quality of life, advancing the profession, and promoting both human dignity and diversity. The preamble is divided into five core values and six fundamental principles. The core values are enhancing human development, honoring diversity, promoting social justice, safeguarding integrity, and practicing competently and ethically. The fundamental principles of ethical behavior are autonomy, nonmaleficence, beneficence, justice, fidelity, and veracity. The ethical purpose section includes stating obligations, identifying relevant considerations, clarifying the nature of responsibilities, serving as a guide for actions, supporting the ACA mission, and processing complaints. Finally, the nine categories of ethical standards are the counseling relationship; confidentiality and privacy; relationships with colleagues; evaluation and assessment; supervision and training; research and publication; counseling by distance, technology, and social media; and resolving issues. See the ACA website (www.counseling.org) for details on these principles and standards, which were adopted in 2014.

Table 9.1 Pay for Various Positions

Careers	Starting Salary	Median Salary	Late-Career Salary	Web Sources
Career counselor	$38,000	$47,000	$59,000	Higher Ed Salaries
Marriage and family therapist	$36,000	$50,500	$75,000	Pay Scale
School counselor	$40,000	$53,000	$72,000	Glass Door
School psychologist	$43,000	$58,000	$88,000	PayScale

American Association for Marriage and Family Therapy

The American Association for Marriage and Family Therapy (AAMFT) has rather lengthy and detailed ethics codes. Four sections include honoring public trust, committing to service and advocacy, seeking consultation, being ethical in making decisions, binding expectations, resolving complaints, aspiring to the core values, and practicing the ethical standards. The core values are expressed as accepting a diverse membership, training therapists with excellence, serving members with excellence, excelling in diversity and equity, having integrity in behavior, and advancing knowledge and innovation. There are eight categories of standards: responsibility to clients, confidentiality, professional competence and integrity, responsibility to students and supervisees, research and publication, technology-assisted professional services, professional evaluations, financial arrangements, and advertising. Visit the AAMFT website (www.aamft.org) for details on the organization's ethics codes, which were adopted in 2015.

National Association of School Psychologists

The four overarching ethical principles promoted by the National Association of School Psychologists (NASP) are respecting dignity and rights, being competent and responsible, relating in an honest manner with integrity, and being responsible to all areas (schools, families, communities, the profession, and society). For details on these principles and their subprinciples, which were adopted in 2010, visit the NASP website (www.nasponline.org).

Salary

As can be seen in Table 9.1, the pay median and range varies for each of the professions discussed in the chapter. The lowest starting salary is approximately $36,000 for MFTs. The highest median salary is approximately $58,000 for school psychologists, who also have the highest salary in later years at $88,000.

Summary

This chapter discussed four distinct careers that are related to each other: career counseling, marriage and family therapy, school counseling, and school psychology. The salary ranges for these professions are similar, with school psychologists at the high end. In some ways, the training of school psychologists is a bit more rigorous and their responsibilities are more weighty. In general, career counselors help late adolescents and adults with career obtainment and satisfaction. MFTs provide emotional and social support to engaged and married couples and families with children. School counselors help children in the school setting by helping choose courses, assisting with college admittance, and providing emotional and social support. School psychologists are responsible for assessing children with special needs and disabilities. They also supervise other school personnel and help with decision making and administration of schools. All of these professions must abide by the ethical principles and guidelines that were described in this chapter.

Reflective Questions

1. What do you think about the role that career counselors play in people's lives? Do you think that more people should have access to career counselors? Why or why not?
2. School counselors spend most of their time helping students pick courses. Do you think it is appropriate for them to also help with social and emotional concerns? Why or why not?
3. MFTs cannot prescribe medicine and must work with a psychiatrist to do so. Do you think this situation is best for MFT clients? Why do you believe as you do?
4. School psychologists do not have much training in school administration and policy. Is it appropriate for them to help school administrators with these duties? Why or why not?

Is This Right for You?

The professions discussed in this chapter have some similarities and some differences. Some of the similarities are the need for a nurturing, responsive, empathetic, and caring personality. You also have to be a good listener and communicator in written and oral form. You have to responsible, ethical, organized, and flexible. You have to think on your feet and be comfortable with variety and unpredictability in your workplace setting. It's also important to learn to take care of your own mental, emotional, and social health. However, these professions will bring you much joy if you want to help people and if you enjoy children and adolescents.

References

Collins, T. P. (2014). Addressing mental health needs in our schools: Supporting the role of school counselors. *The Professional Counselor, 4*(5), 413–416.

DeKruuf, L., & Pehrsson, D.-E. (2011). Schooling counseling site supervisor training: An exploratory study. *Counselor Education & Supervision, 50,* 314–327.

Dixon, A. L., Tucker, C., & Clark, M. A. (2010). Integrating social justice advocacy with national standards of practice: Implications for school counselor education. *Counselor Education & Supervision, 50,* 103–115.

Eagle, J. W., Dowd-Eagle, S. E., Snyder, A., & Holtzman, E. G. (2015). Implementing a Multi-tiered system of support (MTSS): Collaboration between school psychologists and administrators to promote systems-level change. *Journal of Educational and Psychological Consultation, 25,* 160–177.

Fenning, P., Diaz, V., Valley-Gray, S., Cash, R., Spearman, C., Hazel, C. E., . . . Harris, A. (2015). Perceptions of competencies among school psychology trainers and practitioners: What matters? *Psychology in the Schools, 52*(10), 1032–1041.

Garcia-Joslin, J. J., Carrillo, G. L., Guzman, V., Vega, D., Plotts, C. A., & Lasser, J. (2016). Latino immigration: Preparing school psychologists to meet students' needs. *School Psychology Quarterly, 31*(2), 256–269.

Gordon, V. N. (2006). *Career advising: An academic advisor's guide.* Indianapolis, IN: Jossey-Bass.

Hanchon, T. A., & Fernald, L. N. (2013). The provision of counseling services among school psychologists: An exploration of training, current, practices, and perceptions. *Psychology in the Schools*, *50*(7), 651–671.

Karam, E. A., & Sprenkle, D. H. (2010). The research-informed clinician: A guide to training the next-generation MFT. *Journal of Marital and Family Therapy*, *36*(3), 307–319.

Miller, J. K., Todahl, J. L., & Platt, J. J. (2010). The core competency movement in marriage and family therapy: Key considerations from other disciplines. *Journal of Marriage and Family Therapy*, *36*(1), 59–70.

Swank, J. M., & Tyson, L. (2012). School counseling site supervisor training: A web-based approach. *Professional School Counseling*, *16*(1), 40–48.

Vespia, K. M., Fitzpatrick, M. E., Fouad, N. A., Kantamneni, N., & Chen, Y.-L., C. (2010). Multicultural career counseling: A national survey of competencies and practices. *The Career Development Quarterly*, *59*, 54–71.

Wampler, K. S. (2010). Challenge and urgency in defining doctoral education in marriage and family therapy: Valuing complementary models. *Journal of Marriage and Family Therapy*, *36*(3), 291–306.

Young, A., & Kaffenberger, C. (2015). School counseling professional development: Assessing the use of data to inform school counseling services. *Professional School Counseling*, *19*(1), 46–56.

Chapter 10

Behavior Analyst

Behavior analyst is one of the newer and lesser known career paths you can take with a graduate degree in child and adolescent development. You may begin at the level of behavioral technician while still an undergraduate in child and adolescent development. However, to advance in this career you must take a board-certified exam and obtain either a Masters or Doctorate degree. As with other careers in this textbook, you may earn other degrees to follow this career path. Child and adolescent development is an option, as are psychology and education. However, we believe that a degree in child and adolescent development is the best preparation.

In general, behavior analysts work with children who have behavior challenges or behavior deficits, usually supporting children who have autism to help with emotional regulation, communication, and social interaction. However, they can work with other populations, including children with Down syndrome, oppositional defiant disorder, attention deficit disorder, and attention deficit hyperactivity disorder. Behavior analysts work in homes, academic/educational settings, and other settings where peer interactions occur. In addition to working with children and their parents, behavior analysts work with teachers and other professionals (Lang et al.,2010 ; McLaughlin, Denney, Snyder, & Welsh, 2012). Most of their work, but not all, is based on behavioristic theory, also called learning theory in some academic circles. They make and administer behavior charts and shape the behavior of their clients. They promote learning in the natural environment and foster positive social interactions. They are usually trained and work collaboratively (Kelly & Tincani, 2013), meaning that they train with others and work with teachers, parents, and other caregivers.

There exists a career ladder for this field and annual salaries can reach up to $90,000 in some areas of the country. The entry-level position is usually a behavior therapist or behavior technician. At this level, you implement behavior plans that are already created for you. Next is a behavior analyst, which usually requires a Bachelors or Masters degree. To progress further, the ladder, a MA, PhD, or EdD are necessary. Additionally, board certification is a requirement for the highest rungs of the career ladder. This is similar to the exams that physicians and lawyers are required to take. Next steps along the career ladder are program supervisor, where you begin creating the behavior programs, and clinical program manager/ behavior analyst where you supervise and train a number of people and assure the quality of the created behavior programs and their implementation. As with other professional positions, you must maintain your certification and keep up your education on the latest trends.

Needed Characteristics and Abilities

In order to be a behavior analyst, you must want to work with children who have autism or other special needs one-on-one. You have to be able to communicate with the children's parents as well. You must be organized in order to manage information for various clients, and you have to be flexible and be able to work independently. In order to make it to the higher rungs of the career ladder, you will need management skills—and you must also be persistent. You may have to take the certification test more than once in order to obtain certification to become a board certified behavior analyst.

Settings for Positions

Behavior analysts can work in various settings and environments, including schools, hospitals, and private homes. They can work for both for-profit and nonprofit agencies. For example, they could work for a Shriner's Hospital for Children, or in a public school setting. Some behavior analysts work for private companies and drive to homes of clients to work with the children and their families. Behavior analysts can also work for nonprofits, such as the March of Dimes, or governmental regional centers. Wherever children need behavioral intervention, you can find a behavior analyst.

Obtaining Board Certification

The Behavior Analyst Certification Board (BACB) certifies all behavior analysts in the United States and around the world. At minimum, you must have an acceptable graduate degree with an approved sequence of coursework. The graduate degree may be a Masters or Doctorate. In addition to your graduate work in child and adolescent development, you may want to get a graduate degree in psychology or education as well. When obtaining your graduate degrees, be sure that the sequence of your coursework is approved. You can ask the BACB to conduct a preliminary review of your graduate education, if necessary. The 2012 course content requirements on the BACB website (www.bacb.com) state that 270 hours of coursework are required in all (see Table 10.1).

You must also complete 3,250 hours of supervised experience (see Table 10.2). After completing all coursework and experience, you apply to take the BCBA exam. You must submit paperwork and meet the criteria. This is a very rigorous 150-question exam with two main content areas: Basic Behavior Analytic Skills and Client-Centered Responsibilities. More information on the content areas is provided in Table 10.3. The rigor of this

Table 10.1 BCBA Course Content Requirements

Course Content Areas	New Requirements	
	Ethical and Professional Conduct	45 hrs
	Concepts and Principles of Behavior Analysis	45 hrs
Research Methods in Behavior Analysis	Measurement (Including Data Analysis)	25 hrs
	Experimental Design	20 hrs
Applied Behavior Analysis	Identification of the Problem & Assessment	30 hrs
	Fundamental Elements of Behavior Change & Specific Behavior Change Procedures	45 hrs
	Intervention & Behavior Change Considerations	10 hrs
	Behavior Change Systems	10 hrs
	Implementation, Management and Supervision	10 hrs
	Discretionary	30 hrs
	Total	**270 hrs**

Source: Behavior Analyst Certification Board (2012).

Table 10.2 BACB-Appropriate Experience

Requirement	BCBA
Supervised Independent Fieldwork	
Hours of Experience	1,500 hours
Length of Supervisory Period	2 weeks
Minimum # of Contacts per Supervisory Period	1 contact
Minimum Amount of Supervision per Supervisory Period	5% of total hours
Practicum	
Hours of Experience	1,000 hours
Length of Supervisory Period	1 week
Minimum # of Contacts per Supervisory Period	1 contact
Minimum Amount of Supervision per Supervisory Period	7.5% of total hours
Course Grade	Official documentation reflects a passing grade (C or better) in all experience courses.
Intensive Practicum	
Hours of Experience	750 hours
Length of Supervisory Period	1 week
Minimum # of Contacts per Supervisory Period	2 contacts
Minimum Amount of Supervision per Supervisory Period	10% of total hours
Course Grade	Official documentation reflects a passing grade (C or better) in all experience courses.

Source: Behavior Analyst Certification Board (2016)

Table 10.3 BCBA Exam Content and Structure

Content Area	Number of Questions
Basic Behavior Analytic Skills	
A. Measurement	15
B. Experimental Design	11
C. Behavior Change Considerations	3
D. Fundamental Elements of Behavior Change	26
E. Specific Behavior Change Procedures	15
F. Behavior Change Systems	8
Client Centered Responsibilities (will include at least two questions addressing ethics per section)	
G. Identification of the Problem	14
H. Measurement	9
I. Assessment	12
J. Intervention	23
K. Implementation, Management, and Supervision	14
Total Number of Questions	**150**

Source: Behavior Analyst Certification Board. (2017).

exam requires serious amounts of time studying and prepping. It is much like other professional exams taken in the fields of medicine and law.

Real-Life Interviews

Before going further, let us look at some real-life examples of these careers. We will read about Cherie first, as she is a recently certified behavior analyst in a supervisory position who began her work in England. Then we will read about Kristina, who has a supervisory position as a behavior analyst clinical manager and has always worked in the United States.

Cherie's Interview

Cherie has a BS in education, a MA in human services counseling with two emphases, one in marriage and family counseling and one in behavior analysis, from the Florida Institute of Technology. She obtained board certification as a behavior analyst in February of 2016. She currently works as a senior consultant and provides center-based therapy.

Cherie realized early in life that she wanted to work with children in some capacity. Her mother stayed at home and her father was in the air force. They served as foster parents to infants and also aided adolescents without a supportive home life. Her parents left an impression on her and supported her desire to work with children. She had a fifth grade teacher whom she remembered made her want to teach. In college, she started out wanting to be a schoolteacher until she realized that she did not want to work in a school setting. She sees behavioral therapy as similar to teaching. In her current position she trains employees and clients. At the time of our interview, Cherie had been married for one year and was pregnant with her first child. She did not think that her own family impacted her career in any way.

Cherie's career trajectory actually began in England, where she worked as a behavior technician. She was contracted to directly with families for a year. She then returned to the United States and worked as a behavior technician, then was promoted to program supervisor. After a year at this position, during which she obtained BCBA certification, she was promoted to clinical manager. She stayed in that position for six months, but then moved to Louisiana and became a senior consultant in Louisiana. She has held that position for a year.

In her current position Cherie oversees 12 behavior technicians, each with a 16-client case load. On a typical day she supervises approximately four client sessions to ensure the program goals are implemented, and she visits and communicates with families. She also analyzes data and updates treatment targets by writing new treatment goals.

In terms of key turning points and highlights, Cherie mentioned some experiences which lead her to consider this as a career. Although she had enjoyed her job in England, it was when she returned to the United States that she fell in love with the work and wanted to make it a career. When asked about a highlight in her career, she described one client in particular who was aggressive and nonverbal at the age of three. She taught him to use an assistive communication device, which lead him to becoming a very communicative and happy child.

Some of the joys are always growing and learning, and being accountable for continued growth. Cherie also enjoys supporting the behavior technicians whom she supervises to progress and learn. As she sees it, there are three main challenges to her current position: limited time, supervising difficult staff, and convincing skeptical parents. One challenge is having to prioritize, since there is not enough time to accomplish everything you want to do. Another is supervising staff who work without passion and respond to constructive criticism in a negative way. A final last challenge is convincing parents that behavior therapy is valuable and that they should be helping their children to generalize the behavioral skills to their home environment.

The personal characteristics that help Cherie in her profession include having a passion for helping others, loving to help others with their growth (employees and clients), being adaptable, and being flexible. These skills are necessary, she says, because clients change rapidly and so does the field. You have to be able to work with lots of change on a daily basis.

Kristina's Interview

Kristina lives in California, completed her education in California, and started her career in California. She has a BS in human development and a MA in child development in addition to BCBA certification. Her current position is clinical manager/behavior analyst.

Kristina believes her early life impacted her career decisions. She was the oldest child of three. Her family is blended, because her biological parents divorced and she has a stepfather and step-siblings. At the age of 12, she frequently "parented" her siblings whenever her parents weren't home. This experience taught her how to work with children and it also showed her that she likes to manage and lead people. When she was young, she thought that God wanted her to help others. When she entered college she found a field in which she could do that.

Other influences on Kristina's career have included the joy she finds in helping her clients: children and their families. She once had an experience when a mother found out from an assessment that her child was on the autism spectrum. This particular mother took a deep breath and sighed with relief. Kristina wanted to just hug her. This experience and others make her want to stay in her field and do what she does.

After obtaining her MA in child development, Kristina began working as a behavioral therapist. In December 2012, she accepted a position at the UC Davis Mind Institute as a behavioral interventionist. In April 2014, she became a program supervisor at Easter Seals. In the next year, she obtained BCBA certification and was promoted to clinical manager.

In Kristina's current position as Clinical Manager/Behavior Analyst, she supervises all ABA programs for children diagnosed with autism spectrum disorder from 14 months to emerging adulthood. These programs are implemented in the home, in schools, in other peer-group contexts, and in other natural settings. She supervises and works directly with ABA treatment teams, training them and providing professional development. She consults and provides supervision as the teams enhance the skill development of the children. She also does the initial assessment of the children, reviews data and written reports, and communicates with families.

In terms of highlights and turning points, she described two of them. She helped a child go from being nonverbal and aggressive to being verbal and nonaggressive in two years. He was then able to be mainstreamed in a first grade classroom. She also stated that passing the BCBA exam was quite an accomplishment.

As with any career, there have been challenges. The challenges concern the newness of behavior analytic work. Sometimes a behavior analyst's suggestions are not taken seriously because parents or other caregivers feel the advice goes against accepted norms.

Personal characteristics that help her are a passion for helping children and families, and loving the field she chose. She also says she has good leadership qualities, is rule governed, and detail oriented. She is good at teaching and managing staff.

Career Specifics

Ethics

In 2014, the BACB revised the Professional and Ethical Compliance Code for Behavior Analysts; it was fully implemented on January 1, 2016. This 24-page document is quite detailed and comprehensive. Some of the BACB certification exam questions cover the contents of this code. Since behavior analysis is a newer career option, it is necessary to have strict ethical guidelines for professionals behavior analysts at all levels, from technician to behavioral/clinical Supervisor. The BACB code of ethics 10 content areas that are delineated as follows: 1.0, responsible conduct of behavior analysts, 2.0, behavior analysts' responsibility to clients; 3.0, assessing behavior; 4.0, behavior analysts and the behavior-change program; 5.0, behavior analysts as supervisors; 6.0, behavior analysts' ethical responsibility to the profession; 7.0, behavior analysts' ethical responsibility to colleagues; 8.0, public statements; 9.0, behavior analysts and research; and 10.0, behavior analysts' responsibility to the BACB. The subcategories include avoiding false and deceptive statements, supervisory competence, and promoting an ethical culture. More information about ethics and this profession can be found on the BACB website.

Salary

According to PayScale (2017), behavior analyst pay in the United States can range anywhere from $39,799 to $92,831, with Miami, Florida at the high range and Denver, Colorado at the low range. Salary also varies by workplace setting and type of employer. Working for foundations will result in a lower salary than working for a private company or providing home support services. The lowest compensation at the beginning of your career is $36,093 and toward the end of your career the highest is $91,598. These are averages that include all states and span across your entire career. They are not the range limits. That is why these figures differ from previous ones.

Summary

Child and adolescent development is a good foundation for entering the relatively new field of behavior analysis. Behavior analysts work with children who are on the autism spectrum or have behavior disorders. To move up the career ladder, you must have a MA degree and pass the BCBA exam. It is suggested that you see the BCBA website for up-to-date data and requirements. The pay can be quite good, with salaries of approximately $90,000 per year at the top of the pay scale. However, you have to be able to relate to children, parents, family members, and supervised-staff. You have to know how to train, organize, and manage staff. You also have to have good writing skills.

Reflective Questions

1. Do you think the education type and amount required for this field is appropriate?
2. Do you think the internship and training required for this field is appropriate?
3. Is it all right that behavior analysts sometimes suggest and use practices that are not always in keeping with current trends? What if the suggested practices are effective or if they are ineffective? Does that make a difference?

Is This Right for You?

It may be hard to say whether this is right for you. You have to love working with children and families in this type of setting, home, school, peer group. You have to be organized, and also have strong writing skills. In addition, you must be able to relate to children and their parents. If you want to work with children one-to-one, then this can be right for you. This is especially true if you do not want to be a counselor, therapist, or psychologist. However, please note that you will be working with children with intellectual disabilities and somewhat extreme behavior.

References

Behavior Analyst Certification Board. (2012). *BCBA Course Content Requirements*. Littleton, CO.

Kelly, A., & Tincani, M. (2013). Collaborative training and practice among applied behavior analysts who support individuals with autism spectrum disorder. *Education and Training in Autism and Developmental Disabilities*, 48(1), 120–131.

Lang, R., O'Reilly, M. F., Machalicek, W., Rispoli, M., Shogren, K., Chan, J. M., . . . Hopkins, S. (2010). Review of teacher involvement in the applied intervention research for children with autism spectrum disorders. *Education and Training in Autism and Developmental Disabilities*, 45(2), 268–283.

McLaughlin, T. W., Denney, M. K., Snyder, P. A., & Welsh, J. L. (2012). Behavior support interventions implemented by families of young children: Examination of contextual fit. *Journal of Positive Behavior Interventions*, 14(2), 87–97.

PayScale Human Capital. (2017). *Average salary for certification: board certified behavior analyst*. Seattle, WA.

Chapter 11

Child Life Specialist and Other Health Careers

The job of child life specialist is not well known. This is a health care job where child and adolescent development specialists work in hospitals with sick children or children with sick parents (Kaddoura, Leduc, & Cormier, 2013; Sutter & Reid, 2012). The role of child life specialist has been increasing in recent years and the requirements to prepare for this profession have been changing (Association of Child Life Professionals [ACLP], 2018; Smith, Desai, Sira, & Engelke, 2014; Turner & Fralic, 2009). The duties of a child life specialist are varied and emotionally challenging; these specialists work with young clients and their families in delicate situations. For example, child life specialists often work with infants and their families in the neonatal intensive care unit (NICU) or have to comfort and support children who face end-of-life concerns (Parvin & Dickinson, 2010; Smith, Desai, Sira, & Engelke, 2014).

The best source for discovering what a child life specialist does and the requirements for entering this profession is the ACLP website (www.childlife.org). However, we will share information with you that was current at the time of writing this chapter. We will describe current and future requirements, as well as current duties, and we will include real-life interviews with people who have this position.

Requirements for Becoming a Child Life Specialist

Current Requirements

Currently, there exists a set of requirements for being a Child Life Specialist that will change in 2019. As of this writing, a BA degree with specific coursework, an internship of specific hours, and a passing certification exam score are required. Until 2019, a BA in child and adolescent development with other specific coursework will be acceptable. Coursework needs to include a class in Child Life that is taught by a certified person and covers the following topics: documentation, scope of practice, family-centered care, impact of health care on families, therapeutic play, and preparation. Nine additional course topics must be included from among the following: child development, family development, human development, family dynamics, psychology, counseling, sociology, therapeutic recreation, death and dying, ethics, cultural diversity, medical terminology, and anatomy and physiology. Some courses can be taken on an case-by-case basis in nursing, social work, recreation administration, and education.

Before passing an exam, an internship of 480 hours is also required: these cannot be volunteer, practicum, or paid work hours. In addition, the internship has to be supervised by a certified person and verified with an online or paper form (see Figure 11.1).

These requirements are more flexible than they will be beginning in 2019, and the number of internship hours is currently lower. If you are currently studying child and adolescent development, it is important to review the child life specialist requirements for 2019 to 2011 (see Figures 11.2 and 11.3) and to check the website regularly.

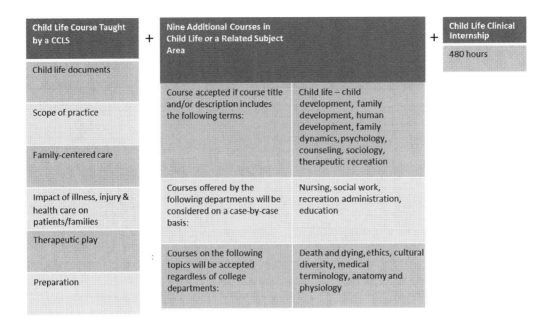

Figure 11.1 Bachelor's Degree Course Requirements Before 2019

Source: ACLP (2017). Eligibility requirements may change over time—please visit the ACLP website for up-to-date information.

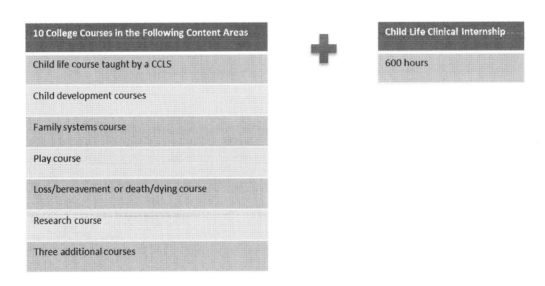

Figure 11.2 Bachelor's Degree Course Requirements January 2019–2022

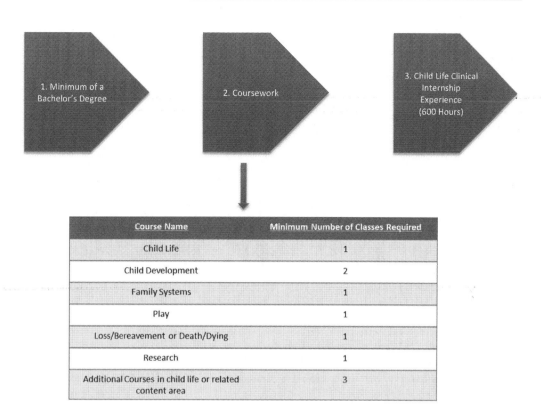

Figure 11.3 Child Life Certification
Eligibility Requirements for Exams After January 2019 and before 2022

Source: Association of Child Life Professionals. (2017). Requirements may change over time—please visit the ACLP website for up-to-date information.

Future Requirements

Starting in 2019, the requirements increase and are less flexible. Specific courses are required and some courses that are accepted now will no longer be accepted. Two or more child and adolescent development classes will be required. Additionally, a family systems course, a play course, a death/dying/loss/bereavement course, and a research course will be required (this is new). As can be expected, a child life specialist class taught by a certified person will still be required, but there will be three additional required courses in related areas; preferred areas are human anatomy/physiology, medical terminology, and ethics. Additional possibilities include psychology, counseling, therapeutic recreation, and expressive therapies. Courses in sociology, social work, nursing, education, or recreation administration will no longer be accepted (see Figures 11.2 and 11.3) An internship will still be required, with a minimum of 600 hours supervised by a certified person. Of course, you will still have to pass the certification exam. After 2022, the requirements will change again.

Duties of a Child Life Specialist

Child life specialists usually work in a hospital with children and their families when the children or the children's parents are ill; a good number work with infants and their families. They assess the situation, document what they find, and provide social and emotional support. Child life specialists usually work in a team of nurses, psychologists, social workers, therapists, and others, to provide care that is developmentally supportive and centered on families. They help to relieve the stress and anxiety of being in the hospital and experiencing health issues, even dealing with death and dying. You can learn more about specific requirements and duties by reading the interviews that follow.

Real-Life Interviews

Angel's Interview

Angel is a child life specialist with a BA in child study and a MA in expressive arts therapy. She states that current requirements include a BA in child and adolescent development and a child life class. She suggests that people with an interest in this career go to the ACLP's website to see current requirements. She has been a child life specialist for 26 years, with 16 of those years as a manager.

Angel believes her early years impacted her career decision, especially an experience when she had eye surgery at 3 years of age. Even before it was routinely allowed, her mother asked the doctor for permission to stay with Angel in the hospital and this was granted. Her family tells this story quite often, because of its significance and meaning. Her mother was a teacher who always worked with children This experience had an impact on Angel's career choice.

Angel's current family life has also impacted her career. She is married, and she had her children after she started her career. Having children made her more empathetic to the families who are her clients. After having children, she was able to put herself in her clients' shoes and gained a better understanding of their plight.

Outside influences on her career include networking, interning, and having a bit of luck. During college, Amy spent some time volunteering and interning at hospitals, where she met influential people in the field. Soon after graduating, Angel met a child life specialist. This person really admired and respected her, and she hired Angel without certification; she had to obtain certification while she was working. Angel says that sort of occurrence would not happen now and she was quite lucky. She mentions also being lucky to have an early director who was a big supporter of family-centered care.

Angel now manages child life specialists. Some of the highlights and turning points in her career journey include working with child heart patients, working with children during illnesses or surgery, initiating bereavement services, and expanding services for her child clients. She has really loved working with children, and she sees the bereavement service as a way to honor children who have passed on. She expanded services for her child clients by offering music therapy and service dogs in hospitals.

Angel wants everyone to know that there is no typical day for a child life specialist or manager. Unexpected tasks come up and many changes can happen to the best planned days in a hospital setting, because of emergencies and other situations. Some of her current duties include managing staff as well as the program and its budget. She also represents the program throughout the hospital. Some of her more detailed tasks include planning and running staff meetings; creating and implementing projects; and supervising and training staff, students, and interns.

As with any profession, there are joys and challenges. It is challenging to adapt to the individual needs of the children and families and personalizing their care. Angel has always tried to make health care as good as it can be. The joys include seeing how resilient children are, as well as empowering children and families and giving them coping skills. She really loves her job.

Characteristics and personality traits that help with this career include problem solving, flexibility, and a positive outlook. Angel states that when you work in a hospital there are many situations that you cannot do much about. There is also grief and stress in abundance. Child life specialists have to stay positive, go with the flow, and discover what can actually be done, if anything, to care of a situation and provide good health care.

Erin's Interview

Erin lives in Colorado and has been a child life specialist for 18 years; for the last five years she has managed child life specialists. She has a BA in human development and family studies and a MA in educational psychology. She really loves children and loves caring for them; in addition, she is married and has children of her own.

Erin has taken care of children since she was 10 or 11 years of age. She believes this early experience influenced her career decision. She says she can really connect with children and youth up to 18 years old. She remembers being in the DMV and seeing a toddler in a car seat who was crying. She began playing with the child, who calmed down. This experience taught her that she can really connect with children.

Erin strongly believes that her current family and career have influenced each other in a bidirectional manner. For example, when she first had children, she was able to work part-time (16–32 hours per week). This allowed her to spend time with her children. She has also been able to use knowledge from her education and career and apply it to her parenting, intentionally teaching her children interpersonal skills and problem solving skills, and developing their emotional intelligence. In addition, being a parent has taught her patience. She knows how the parents of her clients feel, and she can relate to the children, parents, and families. Other influences on her career have included the economy, which was a strong influence on her career trajectory.

Erin has made steady steps up her career ladder. She began as a child life specialist 18 years ago. Early on, she had a chance to co-ordinate interns for a year. She also spent two years as a child life specialist in a hospital operating room. Now, as a manager, her days are 60% managerial and 40% clinical. Her managerial duties are maintaining and enhancing relationships between colleagues and community partners, maintaining a budget, ordering and managing supplies, ordering and managing food, and supervising other child life specialists. Her clinical duties include interacting with and supporting children in the operating room, children whose parents are having operations, and teenagers with eating disorders. Her days are quite variable and she likes it that way. She says it is hard to predict the number of patients that she will see any given day.

Erin has only had two challenges in her career: learning how hospitals work and dealing with many changes in leadership. The joys are many. She especially enjoys working with children and says they are the best part of her job. She also likes to collaborate with interns, students, volunteers, and community members. When working with teams, Erin finds she can go deeper into client cases and see them from multiple perspectives.

Highlights and key turning points in her career include working with an excellent program for her first six years. That program taught her much and exposed her to children with chronic illnesses, such as cystic fibrosis. Children with chronic illnesses made her sad, but also made her more determined to help. Another key turning point was when she began working in the operating room. She really enjoys this placement.

Some of Erin's personal characteristics that make her successful in her job include being responsible, being a high achiever, being friendly, being outgoing, smiling much of the time, and being flexible. Although she is organized and a planner, she can also go with the flow. She likes to make everyone—her clients and her staff—feel noticed, validated, and important. She believes this is the perfect career for those who enjoy variability in their job, as every day is unpredictable.

Desirable Personal Characteristics

Child life specialists work with children and their families in challenging health care situations that sometimes concern death and dying. Being observant, sensitive, and a good listener and communicator are some of the characteristics needed. You also have to be flexible and able to work in variable circumstances—yet also be organized, professional, and ethical. Moreover, we want you to know that you will be working in highly emotional circumstances. You have to find a way to face challenging situations on a regular basis, and to remain cheerful and optimistic, yet realistic.

Workplace Settings

Most child life specialists work in a hospital or another setting related to health care, where children are found, which can be public or private, for-profit hospitals. Some child life specialists work for nonprofit agencies such as March of Dimes, Easter Seals, or Make-A-Wish. Others work in a home or residential facility in affiliation with a hospital where ill children or their parents are receiving long-term care.

Career Specifics

Ethics

As can be seen, ethics are important for child life specialists; a class in ethics is included in the course requirements. Child life specialists also learn about ethics in a child life class taught by certified people. The eight components of a child life specialist's career are listed here and details can be found on the ACLP website:

- infants, children, youth, and families;
- play;
- therapeutic relationships;
- communication;
- theoretical foundations of practice;
- professional collaboration;
- professional standards of practice; and
- research.

Salary

According to the source salary.com on May 30, 2017, the average salary for a regular child life specialist is $49,891, but they can make up to $61,426 or more. However, a person in the position of managing child life specialists can make even more; as with most careers, the salary varies by experience, education, and location.

Other Health Care Professions

Of course, there are other careers in health care with child and adolescent development as an educational foundation—and these careers have their own requirements. Two possibilities are pediatric nurse and pediatric dental hygienist. Here we will briefly describe requirements and job duties of these positions.

A BA degree in child and adolescent development is a good foundation for pediatric nursing. Of course, you will also need a nursing degree. This can be obtained at a community college with an AA degree, as an additional BS degree in nursing, or as a MS degree in nursing. Adding a BA in child and adolescent development can help prepare you by making you more aware of how children develop, grow, and think, which may help you to be more observant, compassionate, empathetic, and understanding.

Pediatric nurses usually work with children in a hospital, medical, health, education, or other setting, although some work in educational institutions or for nonprofit organizations. They assist physicians with helping children be healthy or helping children recover from an illness or other health concern. They are usually supervised by someone with a MD degree and sometimes have to make referrals to a physician. In the school or other non-hospital setting, they may work a bit more independently.

Pediatric dental hygienists can receive either a two-year degree at a community college or a four-year degree at a university. Some for-profit professional training programs also exist. Coupling that education with a BA in child and adolescent development enhances dental hygienists' preparation and practice of their career, helping them to better understand how children develop, grow, and think.

Dental hygienists work in dental offices under the supervision and management of a dentist. They see patients to educate them and provide care such as dental cleanings, assisting dentists with filling cavities, and other similar duties.

Summary

Child life specialists work in hospitals or other health-related settings with children who are ill or with children whose parents are ill. They help relieve the anxiety and stress that come with illness, providing emotional and social support for the children and their parents and families. They provide family-centered care, usually working with a team of nurses, social workers, parent educators, physicians, and other professionals. The training and education requirements for child life specialists are currently changing. In 2019, there will be more requirements for coursework and internship hours. The requirements may change again after 2022. Child life specialists are taught ethics in their coursework and must follow certain standards. Their salary varies by education, location, and experience and can reach above $60,000.

Other health care professions can be enhanced with a degree in child and adolescent development. Pediatric nurses and pediatric dental hygienists are two examples. You must obtain a degree in nursing or dental hygiene to have these careers, but a BA in child and adolescent development will enrich preparation and professional practice. Adding child and adolescent development gives you more academic knowledge about children.

Reflective Questions

1. Should child life specialists have more medical training, or should that type of training just be for nurses and physicians?
2. What standards and ethics should child life specialists abide by at work? Should they take the same oath as physicians?

3. Do you think it should be mandatory for other pediatric health specialists to have some training in child and adolescent development? Why or why not?

Is This Right for You?

When deciding if being a child life specialist is right for you, considering how you manage and express your emotions may be important: child life specialists work with children and their families during challenging times and sometimes deal with death and dying. If you pursue this career you will work in an environment that requires flexibility, optimism, and excellent communication skills (both written and verbal). You may also work in a team, and your opinion and plan will not be the only one considered when deciding how to support the children and families who are your clients. So, does this sound like a career you would like to try? If yes, then becoming a child life specialist is for you.

References

Association of Child Life Professionals (ACLP). (2017). *Eligibility requirements for exams after January 2019 and before 2022.* Retrieved from www.childlife.org/certification/students/.

Association of Child Life Professionals (ACLP). (2018). ACLP website. Retrieved from www.child-life.org/

Kaddoura, M., Leduc, J., & Cormier, K. (2013). Resource collaboration: The benefits of utilizing child life specialists when dealing with pediatric stress. *Educational Research Quarterly, 37*(2), 3–21.

Parvin, K. V., & Dickinson, G. E. (2010). End-of-life issues in US child life specialist programs. *Child Youth Care Forum, 39,* 1–9.

Smith, J. G., Desai, P. P., Sira, N., & Engelke, S. C. (2014). Family-centered developmentally supportive care in the neonatal intensive care unit: Exploring the role and training of child life specialists. *Children's Health Care, 43,* 345–368.

Sutter, C., & Reid, T. (2012). How do we talk to the children? Child life consultation to support the children of seriously ill adult inpatients. *Journal of Palliative Medicine, 15*(2), 1362–1368.

Turner, J. C., & Fralic, J. (2009). Making explicit the implicit: Child life specialists talk about their assessment process. *Child Youth Care Forum, 38,* 39–54.

Chapter 12

Other Career Possibilities

This chapter presents brief descriptions of a number of other career possibilities, plus includes interviews with a children's librarian, children's museum employee, and a children's minister. Some of these careers represent full-time jobs and some represent part-time, supplemental jobs. The intent of this chapter is to present brief descriptions of a number of other options for careers in the field of child and adolescent development that are not very traditional. Let us begin by looking at nanny jobs.

Nanny

Nannies are seen as a traditional job in the field of child and adolescent development. You may be wondering why a BA degree is needed. It is true that you can be a nanny without a degree, but a degree in child and adolescent development will enhance your preparation and performance on the job. You may also be able to obtain one of the higher salaries. It can also be helpful to be bilingual, for example speaking English and French or English and Spanish. Additionally, knowledge of first aid, home environmental safety, and CPR are big pluses to have in your tool kit. In addition to a clean driving record, you will also have to produce a recent TB test and finger print clearance. Since nannies work in private homes and are hired by families, the required prerequisites for the job, conditions of the job, and pay will vary widely.

The duties of a nanny are many. They are the main caretakers for a child or children of a family in the family's private home. They care for the children, provide discipline or guidance for the children, "educate" the children informally, and even parent the children. Sometimes they are responsible for feeding the children, cleaning up after the children, and transporting the children, too. Nannies are virtual or substitute parents. Hours and pay for this position vary widely. Part-time and full-time positions are possible, with salaries ranging from minimum wage a few hours a week to as high as $65,000 to $80,000 or more full-time annual pay. A degree in child and adolescent development and the knowledge gained in the degree program will greatly enhance your chances of getting of full-time, high-paying position.

Nannies may also receive benefits, such as travel with the family, sick days, paid vacation days, health insurance, and such. Additionally, organizations such as Care.com, GoNannies.com, and the International Nanny Association (https://nanny.org) can aid in securing a job with good working conditions. The variety of positions, variety of hours per week, and other flexibilities make this job an attractive one for some child and adolescent development majors.

Children's Ministry

This job is quite an interesting one and may be an option for some child and adolescent development majors. This job is faith-based and a requirement is a belief in a particular religion in addition to having some education and knowledge in child and adolescent development.

Children's ministry personnel work in religious institutions. Their charge varies widely, as they may just help with Sunday (or Saturday) Services and children's religious education, or they could have other duties. They can be involved with specific religious events for children, or with community partnerships, or with the academic education and socialization of young children. Depending on how large the religious institution and Children's ministry staff are, they may have to train staff, recruit and train volunteers, and write rules and policies. They usually have a budget, help with facilities, and act as a liaison with families that attend the religious institution. They may also be involved with writing grants to support their activities. What does the job of Children's ministry leader look in real life? Let us look at an interview with a minister.

Frank's Interview

Frank has a BA in child development and many years in ministry, with more than 10 years involved in some way with children's ministry. Frank is married, with two children of his own. His wife is a nonlicensed social worker in the field of special education, a complimentary vocation that can also be obtained with a degree in child and adolescent development.

Frank believes that his family background impacted his career decision. He grew up regularly attending religious services. He also participated in a lot of activities, such as sports and summer camps. These early experiences provided him with knowledge and understanding that help him with his career duties today.

His current family situation also influences his career. However, Frank sees that influence as mutual or bidirectional. Studying child and adolescent development helped him to raise his children and have a good marriage—but his family has impacted his career, too. Both of his children were born premature. This underscored for him the importance of supporting and educating parents. He saw the importance of his career choice, tasks, and duties. He also realized that he had to support and educate the volunteers he was recruiting as a children's minister.

So, what does a children's minister do? Frank equates his job to being a principal at a public elementary school. Children's ministers are responsible for all activities that involve children at a particular religious institution. His duties vary widely, so flexibility is needed. On a daily basis, Frank could write or select curriculum, oversee and hire full-time and part-time staff, direct camps, direct community outreach events, assist with marketing the ministry, recruit and train volunteers, manage a budget, and perform other general pastoral duties. His general duties include weekly staff meetings, committee work, and counseling church attendees.

So what has been Frank's journey up until this point? In high school, he was active in his church and participated in paid internship programs. This helped him to learn how to be a leader at a young age. In college, he started out as a business major, as both of his parents were business owners. By sophomore year, he realized he did not enjoy the business classes and enjoyed his child psychology and sociology courses more. He then switched schools and decided to major in child development with the goal of becoming an educator, and eventually a school principal. While still in college, he had a job teaching in an afterschool program. When he graduated with his BA, however, his intended teaching credential program was impacted. Instead, he found a job as program director with a youth ministry program called Youth for Christ. He did that job for three years, while still teaching part-time in an afterschool program and interning at his church. Then he spent three years as an associate Sunday School director and 10 years as pastor of children's ministries. During this time he was in charge of Sunday School, teen ministries, summer camp, other camps (sports, music, etc.), child care, and children with special needs. Currently, his role has expanded and he is now pastor of community outreach.

Other influences on his career have been volunteering and interning when he was young. Additionally, discovering his gifts and talents and abilities through personality tests was influential. The most influential experience was being the vice president and president of a professional business fraternity for two years in college. He then really put his gifts to use. He discovered that he was a "servant leader." According to Frank, this type of leader is humble, leads by example, and is not afraid to get down and work in the trenches as well as lead. This type of leader takes care of his or her staff and volunteers and gives them what it takes to succeed.

As with any job, there are challenges. One of the main challenges is the instability and inconsistency of funding throughout the years, since his church is supported by donations. This impacts the amount and quality of children's programming available. The second main challenge is staff and volunteer turnover and training. This is another unpredictable aspect of the job that impacts the programming available.

Of course, there are also joys and highlights in Frank's career journey, including getting to know people who volunteer, as some have become friends. The greatest joy has been watching the children grow, mature, become leaders, and become productive adult members of society that help other children grow or help the community. Also, he sees that his church has been helping the community, as relationships have grown with the city government and local school district.

So what does it take to be a good children's minister? You have to be a good communicator who is an attentive listener and have a relational personality. You also have to have an eye for detail in addition to an eye for structure and be team minded. Most importantly, you need to put others before you and be humble as a servant leader.

Family Lawyer

It is obvious that continued education is necessary for becoming a family lawyer. After obtaining your BA in child and adolescent development, you must take the LSAT, attend law school and earn a JD degree (a minimum of three years), and pass the bar exam. It is also wise to get some experience as a volunteer in a law office and to minor in a field related to law such as history or political science or business. Another route to becoming a family lawyer is becoming a paralegal upon earning your BA. This BA can be in Child and Adolescent Development. However, you must also pass a test. A paralegal is an assistant to a lawyer who helps with research and case preparation. While working as a paralegal, you can complete your JD degree—but that will probably take more than three years to complete.

In general, family lawyers assist with legal matters such as child custody, divorce, alimony, paternity, definition of marriage, domestic violence, and child emancipation. Family lawyers can work in private practice or with a large law firm. When working with a law firm, you can progress from associate to partner (Lawcrossing.com, 2017; Study.com, 2017).

It is very important to be able to communicate, both verbally and in written products. The lion's share of a family lawyer's duties concern communicating. Lawyers write documents and present a client's case verbally in a court of law or during mediation or arbitration. It is also important to manage time and be organized. According to the Bureau of Labor Statistics (2016), the average salary for a lawyer in 2015 was $115,820.

Juvenile Justice

Another career avenue for child and adolescent development majors is juvenile justice. If this area interests you, you may want to double major or at least minor in criminal justice. Alternatively, you may also want to double major or minor in sociology. Some of the juvenile justice positions just require a high school diploma and the passing of some exams. However, a BA degree in child and adolescent development will give you a good foundation.

There are three main career options under juvenile justice, and each has a career ladder. You can go into law enforcement and become a police officer. You can go into corrections and work in a juvenile jail or prison system, or become a probation officer and work to rehabilitate and monitor juvenile offenders after their release. Sometimes juvenile probation officers work with youth in a residential setting while they are preparing for trial. So, in these jobs you are working with troubled youth (The balance.com, 2017; Study.com, 2017). According to the Bureau of Labor Statistics (2016), the average yearly salary for these types of positions in 2015 was $40,530. The high end of the salary range includes a yearly salary of about $100,000 dollars.

Adoption Caseworker

Adoption caseworkers find suitable families for children without parents or children whose parents are declared legally unfit (Study.com, 2017). To determine suitability of the adopting family, they do consultations, interviews, and evaluations of the new home and family. They may also do some training of the new family units and post-adoption counseling and home visiting. Usually a BA degree in child and adolescent development and the passing of some tests is all that is required, but some states require specific licensing in social work and or a MA degree for adoption caseworkers. In 2015, the median annual salary was $42,350 (Bureau of Labor Statistics, 2016).

Foster Care Parent

Foster care parents temporarily care for children whose parents are unable to do so because of health reasons or legal issues. These children have often been neglected and sometimes abused by their birth parents. The major goal of the foster parent system is to one day reunite children with their family. Although parenting is a full-time job, foster parenting is mostly a side career. Some people foster other children because they love children and parenting and they want to make extra money. Others become foster parents in hopes of some day adopting one of the children. Still others want to give back to society.

Foster care parent agencies usually share responsibility for providing the children's needs. These agencies supervise, monitor, and train the foster care parents. Foster care parents must follow many rules concerning the children in their care. For instance, they must keep good records of education progress and health of the child. They have to provide recreation and appropriate clothing. Everything a foster care parent does is coordinated and managed by the foster care agency. Although a BA is not required for this position, a BA in child and adolescent development is good preparation.

Nonlicensed Social Work

There are social work-type positions that do not require a license. You can work in these jobs with a BA or MA in child and adolescent development. One of the main positions in this category is a case manager in child protective services, which are governmental agencies. Case managers manage and coordinate a number of child abuse and/or neglect cases. They do investigations of abuse/neglect cases and train parents (foster, biological, and adoptive). They analyze data and write reports. They also make suggestions to the court concerning the children, such as if and when they should be returned to their family of origin.

Another nonlicensed social work career possibility is life skills coach. In this position, you work with low-income children and families to help them lead positive and productive lives. You help with mediating, parenting, and job hunting, and provide referrals to services in the surrounding residential area, among other duties. You also conduct workshops, analyze data, and write reports. A degree in child and adolescent development at the BA or MA level can help you obtain this position.

There nonlicensed social work positions in educational settings, too. For example, you can be a parent liaison or home visitor. As with other similar positions, a BA or MA in child development is good preparation for the job. In these positions you can expect your salary to range from approximately $30,000 to $60,000. This depends on the number of years you spend in the career and the geographic location of the job.

Museum Positions

There are different types of museums and various positions at museums that are suitable for people with a degree in child and adolescent development. Docents (paid or volunteer) give tours or protect exhibits at a museum. Curators decide what is placed in the museum exhibits. Depending on how big the museum is and the geographic location, the salaries of curators run from $35,000 to $80,000 a year. These are general museum jobs, but there are other more specific museum jobs related directly to the field of child and adolescent development.

For instance, you can be the executive director of a children's museum, which is like being the president or CEO. You are in charge of operating the museum, managing staff, hiring and training staff, and ultimately ensuring the success of the museum. You can also be the education program manager with a degree in child and adolescent development. You will be in charge of education programs and either providing them all yourself or hiring others to do so. Most education programs are for children, but some are for adults. Since museums are usually nonprofit organizations, you would have to fundraise and manage a budget. You may also have to write grants proposals. Jobs such as these range from approximately $45,000 to $100,000.

Finally, you could be a researcher at a large, well-funded museum. A MA or PhD in child and adolescent development is usually required. This person would be involved in grant writing, evaluating education programs, and the securing outside contracts. They can also assist with writing curriculum and deciding which exhibits to borrow. Additionally, they assist with writing annual reports and analyzing other relevant data. To explain more about this position, an interview follows.

Gary's Interview

Gary has a BA in Psychology and a MA in Developmental Psychology and a PhD in educational psychology. He currently fills two positions: research fellow at a children's museum (which he has held for four years) and postdoctoral researcher at a major university (where he has been for about a month). In the past, he has held a wide variety of positions such as nanny, preschool teacher, and adjunct professor. These positions helped him to finance his education and support his family. He is married, with a young daughter. This interview focuses on his position as a research fellow at a children's museum.

Gary is very emphatic when discussing the influence of his family of origin on his career trajectory and choice. His parents did not go to college, but they were hard workers who impressed upon Gary the value of hard work. He also remembers being in a lot of gifted and talented programs growing up, which enhanced his learning and made him appreciative of education.

Gary's current family also has influenced his career trajectory. He moved to another state to set down roots and be with his current wife. He also thinks about letting his daughter see him do a job and career that is something that he loves and a job for which he has a lot of passion.

Other influences on Gary's career are mentors during his BA and MA programs. He had fantastic and supportive mentors. In addition, during his PhD program, he learned how to navigate politics in work situations.

So, what does a research fellow in a museum do? Gary's job is similar to that of a researcher in other nonprofit organizations. His tasks change on a daily basis and depend on the grants and contracts that the museum has. Some of the tasks he performs include conducting literature reviews, presenting research to teachers and stakeholders, conducting professional development for Pre–K through 12th grade teachers, developing curricula, developing assessments for Pre–K through fourth grade teachers, creating a database of school enrichment activities, writing policy briefs and white papers, analyzing research trends, managing undergraduate students, and managing research assistants. He also writes grant proposals and secures contracts.

Gary has had several key turning points, highlights, and joys. He really loves working with children and helping others. He enjoys interdisciplinary research and the fact that he has worked in a variety of contexts. He is really excited that his first journal article has been highly cited and referenced. The two main turning points in his life have been not finishing his first MA in environmental sustainability and meeting his current wife. When he was studying for his first MA he grew spiritually, but realized he wanted to study more about children than the environment. Meeting his future wife centered him and led him to move to another state to put down roots.

He has experienced two main challenges: learning to navigate work politics and to say "no" to protect himself from overwork. Each challenge has taught him a lot and made him stronger.

The personal characteristics that have made him successful are being hard working, flexible, open to new experiences, and very persistent. He has also made a conscious choice to always maintain a spiritual dimension in his teaching, research, and personal interactions.

He has always chosen to interact with others with integrity and grace, even if it meant his career would not advance along a traditional path.

He believes his work is a calling for him. He believes he is having an impact on the world by inspiring his students and giving new information to the world through his research. He also wants to be a model for his daughter when it comes to loving your work.

Recreational Therapy

Another career available to child and adolescent development majors is recreational therapist, especially working with children in this capacity. If this is your goal, we suggest that you minor in recreational therapy or obtain a double major. However, having a degree in child and adolescent development will help you to understand children better and give you an enhanced foundation for this career. You may also have to obtain a state license or certification from the National Council of Therapeutic Recreation.

Recreational therapists can work in a variety of settings, such as schools, medical facilities, community centers, or nonprofit organizations. They nurture their patients with specifically tailored recreational activities that impact their patients' minds, bodies, and spirits. These activities may be arts and crafts, field trips, dances, sports, theatrical performances, or other activities. The patients of recreational therapists usually have a disease, injury, or disability. According to the Bureau of Labor Statistics (2017), the medium income from 2016 is $46,410.

Occupational Therapy

Similar to recreational therapists, occupational therapists work with individuals who are sick, injured, or disabled, in a variety of settings. In addition to schools, hospitals, community organizations, and nonprofits, occupational therapists can work in nursing homes, home health settings, and private offices. Occupational therapists help their patients recover physical and mental functions and skills. These skills allow their patients to live independently and perform daily tasks and work.

The education needed for this career is a MA in occupational therapy. However, a BA in child and adolescent development can be your start. You may want to minor in biology or double major. Alternatively, you could minor in general science. In any case, it is important to take the prerequisites necessary to enter the MA program in occupational therapy. Also, it is important to have volunteer experience in an occupational therapy setting. In 2016, the median salary for occupational therapists was $81,910 (Bureau of Labor Statistics, 2017).

Children's Librarian

Children's librarians usually work in schools (public or private), or local community libraries. Most school librarians are former teachers, but not all. Librarians in the community do not usually have teaching experience, but may have some teaching experience. The typical degree requirement is a MA in library sciences. Before obtaining that degree, a BA in child and adolescent development is a possible foundation. You may want to minor in library sciences or double major. You may also want to take courses in children's literature and/or multi-cultural children's literature. Librarians choose which books the library carries for its patrons and students. They also oversee and manage and train paid staff and volunteers. An example of a staff position that is supervised by a librarian is the coordinator of children's services. Librarians also plan programming for children and adolescents, liaison with the community, and manage library technology use and initiatives. Pay for librarians varies widely depending on the setting, job title, and years of experience.

Sally's Interview

Sally is a children's librarian at a private lower school (pre-K through fifth grade). She has a BA in psychology, a MS in education and special education, and five specialist credentials. She taught elementary and middle school for a number of years before becoming a librarian. Sally has been a children's librarian for five years.

Sally believes that both her family of origin and her current family have impacted her career choice. She is from the Midwest and has German and Irish roots. She is married, with three grown children (two sons and a daughter). All of this she believes has impacted her career in some way.

Other influences have been her background in reading diagnostics and her 12 years as a mentor teacher. She loves teaching reading, reading, and mentoring other teachers. She loves collaborating with her colleagues, too. All of this brought her to her current position and influenced her career path to this point.

Sally's weekly schedule has some flexibility. There are 13 classes (Pre-K through 5th) in the school where she works. All of those classes have a regularly scheduled time to come to the library each week. Some extra library time may be scheduled if the students have a special project. She tries to get to know each student as an individual and help with reading skills, strategies, reading comprehension, and library skills. She also wants to foster a love of reading. Additionally, she hosts special events concerning reading, including author readings, Book Bonanza, and Read Across America. She also schedules and prepares for meetings in the library. The physical appearance of the library is also her responsibility. She cleans, organizes, and shelves books. She noted that each day approximately 2,000 books are in circulation at any given time.

The major highlight of her journey to librarian was during her teacher training. She learned the Cognitive Curriculum for Young Children at Vanderbilt University. This enhanced her ability to mediate children's learning and question them in a way that enhanced their learning. This, she believes, brought about cognitive change in her students.

The joys of being a children's librarian, according to Sally, are watching struggling readers thrive, watching former students graduate, seeing students choose to become teachers and/ or librarians themselves, collaborating with others, and interacting with students from all grade levels. The only challenge has been finding the time to do everything she wants to do for her students. However, she loves her current position. This is because she is given the tools she needs to do well and she is allowed to do what she feels is best for her students.

The personal characteristics that have helped her along her career are many. She has a drive to be professional and do well in her career. In addition, she is quite organized and is a perfectionist. She enjoys working on teams and collaborating. She loves her job. She has had a wide variety of experiences. All of this helps her in her current position as children's librarian.

Summary

This chapter briefly introduced positions that are obtainable with a degree in child and adolescent development. These positions are not the ones that come to mind most often and they require extra academic preparation, but they are obtainable nevertheless. Child and adolescent development makes a good foundation for these careers. You may experience a number of career options with this educational foundation and can make changes along your career journey. Hopefully, this is evident to you now. So at one point, you can be a nanny or teacher or librarian. Then you can change or do something related after extra education, such as lawyer or occupational therapist. Your options are numerous.

Reflective Questions

1. What are the three most intriguing career options in this chapter for you? Why?
2. After reading this chapter, are you more interested or less interested in the field of child and adolescent development? Why or why not?
3. Which of the three interview vignettes from this chapter intrigued you the most? Why?

Is This Right for You?

Did any of the jobs profiled in this chapter strike your fancy or seem like a career possibility? Some of these you may not have thought about, but are now considering. Do you have what is needed for occupational therapy? Do you have the organization and people skills needed for almost any job? Can you handle juvenile justice or social work? These are questions you must answer. Chapters 13 and 14 will help you reflect a bit more on yourself and a bit more on initiating a career journey. Continue reading to learn more about yourself and choosing a career.

References

The balance.com (2017). Juvenile Correction Officer.

Bureau of Labor Statistics, U.S. Department of Labor OOH, 2016–2017 edition, Adoption Caseworker, Juvenile Correction Officer, Lawyer, Occupational Therapists, Recreational Therapists.

Lawcrossing.com (2017). Family Attorney Job Description.

Study.com (2017). Adoption Caseworker, Family Lawyer, Juvenile Correction Officer.

Part 3

Discovering Your Path

Chapter 13

Reflections on Self

This chapter will guide you to reflect on yourself in terms of personality and ability, and to reflect on and explore the various careers discussed throughout the textbook. Hopefully, this reflection will help you in narrowing your career choices. In this chapter, and the companion website, our goal is to guide you in discovering a career path that fits you and your situation. In this chapter we begin by asking you to reflect on yourself and your current situation. Next, we ask you to focus on and contemplate your goals and plans. Then we set you on a journey to utilize current career assessment tools to discover your abilities, characteristics, interests, and values. Finally, you can think once again about your career possibilities and narrow down your choices. So, let us begin this journey on the search for a career match in terms of a career path and choice.

Reflecting on Yourself and Your Current Situation

As you have been reading this textbook you have been exposed to several different careers and several interviews with professionals in the field of child and adolescent development. You have learned about the fields of ECE and elementary school teaching, and discovered careers such as applied behavior analysts and children's ministry. You have learned that career paths are not always linear: sometimes they take unforeseen twists and turns. You have learned about the types of characteristics and abilities needed for the various careers, as well as the academic degrees, certificates, and credentials. When you started this textbook, you may have had different ideas about your career choice and path than you do now. So, we would like you to think about yourself and current situation right now. If you think about it, you have already started your career journey. Whether you are just beginning postsecondary education, in a graduate program, or somewhere in the middle, you are currently on your career path. You may even be midcareer or ending one career to begin another. Wherever you may be on your career path, by reading this textbook you are taking another step on your path and climbing another rung on the career ladder. Since you have taken in a lot of new information, we want you to pause and think about yourself and your current situation seriously and thoroughly.

Self-Reflection

We suggest that you begin with informal self-reflection and think about how well you know yourself. In traditional child and adolescent development literature, Erikson (1963, 1982) states that identity formation is a task of the adolescent and perhaps the emerging adult. However, some people form an identity without being aware of the process. In order to choose a career, it is best to know yourself well and to know how others see you. When it comes to knowing yourself and choosing a career, it is best to know your characteristics and abilities, as well as values and interests. Moreover, it is best to have an honest assessment of these characteristics, abilities, values, and interests. We present here an informal method of self-reflection (See Table 13.1).

Make a list of five to 15 of your dominant personality characteristics as you see them. Dominant personality characteristics are traits that you demonstrate most of the time and/

Table 13.1 Self-Reflection

Characteristics
Strengths
Weaknesses
Abilities/Skills
Core
Peripheral
Values/Interests
Core
Peripheral

or that people think about first when thinking about you. Divide this list into strengths and weaknesses, and enter that information into Table 13.1. Then make a list of five to 15 abilities and/or skills you have and divide this list into core skills and peripheral skills. Core skills are the ones that are the strongest in your repertoire and peripheral skills are those that are not as strong or those that may need some assistance from others. Enter that information into the table. Last, make a list of five to 15 values and interests. Then divide this list into core and peripheral values and interests, and enter that information into the table. Remember, to think and reflect informally first. This is just a process that we suggest to aid you on your journey. Later on in the chapter, we will present more formal tools for assessing your characteristics, abilities, values, and interests. Take your time at this step, as it is an important beginning to your journey.

After you have done this, ask a few people who you believe know you well to go through the same process. Ask them to list your characteristics, abilities/skills, values, and interests. Next examine all of the lists to look for congruence and incongruence. Then discuss the lists with those few people individually or in a group and see what you have learned about yourself. Did the few close family members or friends or classmates help you discover more about yourself that you did not know? Was there a lot of congruence or a lot of surprises? We want you to remember that this is just informal information, but it is useful. This information helps you to gain a more realistic and holistic picture of yourself. However, there are more formal tools for assessing and describing this same information that will be revealed later on in the chapter.

Current Situation

Now that you have reflected on yourself, please take some time to think about your current situation (See Table 13.2). Experiences and education are important.

You may be a freshman in college or a seasoned veteran in the field of child and adolescent development who is changing direction. You may be single or you may have a spouse or significant other and children. Additionally, your level and type of education may vary. Perhaps, you are a college freshman or a recent child and adolescent development Bachelor degree recipient who is on the way to law school, nursing school, or maybe even seminary if wanted for children's ministry. When thinking about your current situation, you also want to think about current resources. How much time, energy, attention, and money do you have to get you to your career goals? You may also want to assess your social capital, as a resource (Sandoval-Lucero, Maes, & Klingsmith, 2014). Social capital is the amount of influence you have in the social world and the networking relationships and supportive relationships you have in the social world. In other words, who do you know who can support you and connect you to others? How much influence do you have in your social world? Location is another consideration. Where do you live? Do you want to move? What are the requirements for your chosen profession in your current or chosen place of residence? When assessing your current situation, we suggest you evaluate your current work situation and experience, your current configuration of loved ones who support you and need support from you, your current amount and type of education, what type and how much education is needed for the desired position, your current resources (financial, social, emotional), and your current and preferred location. It is important to consider the support you get from your workplace as this is needed for you to survive and thrive. Also, consider the climate and geographic traits that you prefer. Do you want four seasons or mountains? Do you want family near or within traveling distance?

Table 13.2 Current Situation

Related Work Experiences		
Volunteer		
Internship		
Paid		

	Educational Accomplishments	Educational Goals
AA Degree **What Field?**		
BA Degree **What Field?**		
MA Degree **What Field?**		
Doctoral/Professional **Degree** **What Field?**		
Certificates or Licenses?		

A Summary of Resources

As mentioned earlier, your resources are your social capital, time, energy, attention, and money. Think about whom you know who can open doors for you, support you, and mentor you. Think about your time, energy, and attention. As well, you must think about money. How much money do you have? How much money can you get through grants, fellowships, and scholarships? Grants and scholarships are given to you and have criteria. Fellowships may contain a work component. You do not have to pay any of these back.

How much money have you borrowed already? How much can and should you borrow now and in the future? Loans are serious considerations. It is advisable to consult an educational coach, career coach, life coach, or accountant on financial matters. If you are currently in an educational institution, then you can consult the financial aid office. Last, realistically consider your social capital, including institutions and people: these contacts can assist you as you pursue your career in child and adolescent development. You should take a realistic look at your total current situation and then begin examining your goals and making your plans. This is how we suggest you think about your current situation, informally, before you articulate your goals and plans. We suggest the following process for assessing your current situation in depth.

The Process

First, examine your past and current work situation. What volunteer, internship, or paid work experiences have you had that are related to the field of child and adolescent development? In which of these experiences are you currently engaged? How long have you engaged in these experiences? How much responsibility do you have? Are you supervising others? Has the amount of responsibility and supervision increased? All experiences from babysitting and working in a grocery store play center to teaching infants and teaching college students should be considered as experience. Variation in experience is important, too. So, think about babysitting children with autism, being a camp counselor, or volunteering in a children's hospital. This step is important because you need experience in a line of work to get a good position. It is also important because it gives you information about what skills and abilities and preferences you have now.

Now assess your current educational accomplishments. Have you completed an associate of arts degree, a bachelor of arts degree, master of arts degree, or doctoral degree in child and adolescent development? Have you completed a degree in a related field, such as applied psychology, developmental psychology, ECE, educational psychology or social psychology? Did you obtain any awards, certificates, or licenses while becoming educated? Have you been formally accepted to the next level of educational progress? Remember all of the work experiences you have had that occurred during your education, too. For instance, did you volunteer or have an internship or service learning experience related to your education in a class? Maybe you have a BA or have almost finished with a BA, but you have a goal to get an MA or PhD? Be sure to include your goals and aspirations in your assessment of your current educational situation. It is important to know what your overall educational goals and aspirations are. The SMART (Specific, Measurable, Action-Oriented, Realistic, and Timely; Dembo, 2008) goal process can be helpful here. Your goals and plans should be specific, measurable, action-oriented, realistic, and timely.

After evaluating your educational accomplishments and goals, think about resources. We suggest taking a realistic look at your time, energy/attention, money, and social capital (see Table 13.3).

A realistic examination of resources will help you to determine if your educational goals and career aspirations are reachable. Use Table 13.3 or create your own chart or graphic and take a realistic accounting of your resources. Make a chart of your time on a daily, weekly, and monthly basis. Be sure that you include essentials such as sleep, fun, relaxation, and exercise in your time chart. Although some people find that their current work is pleasurable, others may find it to be a chore. Then assess energy and attention. When do you have the most energy, attention, and focus? Are you more energetic and attentive in

Table 13.3 Resources

Time (Hours)		
Daily		
Weekly		
Monthly		
Energy and Attention		
When are you most focused?		
Highest amount of time you are able to give		
Length of time		
Money		
Current amount of assets		
Possible grants/scholarships/fellowships		
Possible loans		
Current amount of debt		
Ideal debt ceiling		
Social Capital		
	Existing	**Potential**
People		
Institutions		

the mornings, afternoons, or evenings? How often and for how long can you give serious energy and attention to a task each day? Money is the next resource to consider. How much do you have that you can devote to career exploration and furthering your education? Do you fit the criteria for a grant, scholarship, or fellowship? Can you take out a loan? How much debt do you have already? What is the ceiling on the amount of debt you want to acquire? Then there is social capital to consider. Who and/or what institutions and contacts are in your network? Who can give you resources or help you acquire more resources? Another current consideration is location. Where do you live and where would you want to live? What are the rules, regulations, and requirements for your dream job in your dream location? All of these factors are to be considered as you make a decision about the next stage in your journey to your ideal career in child and adolescent development.

Determining Your Goals and Plans

When determining your career goals and plans, we suggest that you think about both career goals and about personal goals. What is your ideal career and when can you realistically start it? What education will be needed? What are your personal plans and goals for your life? How do these separate sets of goals mesh with each other?

Career Goals

Think about how much education you have and want to complete and in what time frame. Also, think about what types of tasks you want to complete at work and in what setting you want to work. Do you want to work part-time or full-time, and for how many years? Do you want to change positions during your career in order to increase your earning

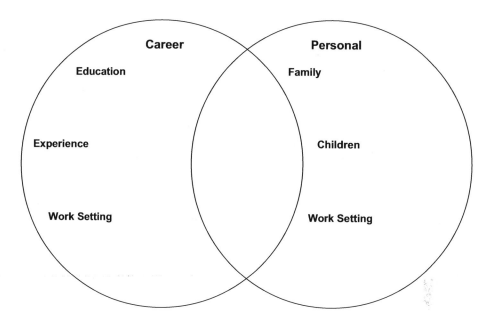

Figure 13.1 Goals and Plans

potential or in order to provide for variety? Some people want variety in their career positions and that is what drives them. How long do you plan on staying in each position? These are the questions to consider when making career goals and plans. Figure 13.1 gives you a diagram where you can write your goals and plans. The SMART goal system mentioned previously can help with this as well.

Personal Goals

Figure 13.1 includes personal goals, because these are important when planning for your career. Do you want to have children? How many children do you want to have? Do you want to marry or remarry?? How many hours do you want to work a day? In what setting do you want to work? These are some personal goals that impact your career goals by influencing your happiness, joy, and commitment.

You have thought about yourself, your current situation, and your career goals and plans in a systematic manner. The next section of this chapter takes you on a journey to formally assess your characteristics, values, and interests with some of the standard career exploration instruments in the field. The answers you have now for yourself, after the informal assessments, may or may not be the same answers you have after you complete the formal standard assessments. These answers may differ depending on how self-aware you are and how detailed and thorough your self-reflections were. So, let us now explore some formal, standard career tools.

Standard Career Assessment Tools

This section of the chapter will introduce you to various career assessment tools. We are not endorsing any of the assessments. Please note that other assessments exist besides the ones mentioned in this chapter.

Myers-Briggs Type Inventory

The Myers-Briggs Type Inventory (MBTI; Myers, 1962). The MBTI assesses personality-based perception and judgment preferences. "Perception" in this assessment is defined as awareness, and "judgment" is defined as the process you use to make conclusions. A person's perception and judgment preferences create 16 unique personality styles based on four basic decisions. Are you an introvert or extrovert? Do you sense information or do you interpret information? Do you make decisions with logic or feeling? When making conclusions, do you arrive quickly at a judgment or stay open? The 16 unique personality styles created from answering these questions are all valuable and none are seen as better than another. This test simply helps you to understand and consider differences in your own individual preferences; it provides a wealth of information to guide you in making your career choice.

The MBTI was first developed in the 1940s and has been revised. A multitude of research has been completed on it to support its reliability and validity. ("Reliability" is measuring the same concepts in the same way over and over again, while "validity" is measuring the concepts accurately). People in many cultures and nations have taken this test. This suggests that the MBTI as a measure is valid for a great number of people. It is a standard in child and adolescent development and completing it can assist you in self-reflection and career choice.

The Personalities

There exists another test of personality that is simply titled "The Personalities," and is the creation of Fred Littauer (Littauer & Littauer, 2006). Taking this test results in a profile of strengths and weaknesses of your personality type. According to this test, there are four personality types and some personality types may be paired. All personality types have strengths and weakness. The literature on The Personalities suggests that having two personality pairs that usually do not go together or having a combination of three or four personality types is the result of masking. According to The Personalities, masking occurs when we learn to act in a certain way that is not our true, natural self. "Masking" is also a formal term in child and adolescent development theory that can be defined as when a behavior covers or takes the place of another behavior (Johnson, 2007).

The Personalities author wants it to be an aid in helping you understand yourself and others. It also includes work and friendship categories of a person's attributes in his or her personality profile. Other purposes of The Personalities are to get along with others better and be a better parent. The most distinguishing and unique feature of this test is that all of the personality types have strengths and weaknesses.

Strong Interest Inventory Assessment

The next assessment to be described has been in existence for more than 80 years. The Strong Interest Inventory Assessment (SIIA) is a comprehensive test of a person's interests that was revised by CPP in 2012. The SIIA contains 30 basic-interest scales, 260 occupational scales, and five personal style scales. The interest scales form specific patterns that match with the occupational scales. The general occupational scale themes are based on John Holland's framework (Holland, 2014), which is discussed in "The Career Key Test" section later on in the chapter.

The SIIA has very stable reliability and validity scores (CPP, 2004, 2012). It is normed with a representative sample in terms of ethnicity and race and other demographics. In other words, the scores from this measure are based on a diverse population of people. It is used all over the world and highly respected by psychologists and professionals in the field. Users find the results to be easy to comprehend. Sometimes employers and employees use it in combination with the MBTI for a complete profile, which is beneficial for both employers and employees because it assists with goal setting and accomplishment, motivation, and planning.

Campbell Interest and Skill Inventory

The Campbell Interest and Skill Survey (CISS) by David Campbell (1992) measures both interests and skills as part of a standard career assessment tool. However, it is being placed in this section of the chapter, as it is the only one to be mentioned that measures skills. The CISS is comprehensive, with 200 interest items and 160 skill items that parallel each other. There are 29 basic scales that reduce to seven categories of orientation scales. Along with a profile score, this assessment also results in a career plan. This assessment has been translated into Spanish.

The CISS has much research data to support it. This research is based on norms from more than 5,000 adults, yet the CISS can be used with people as young as 15 years old. People who take this assessment receive a comprehensive profile that contains numbers, graphic depictions, and written narratives.

Career Beliefs Inventory

The next assessment to be described is newer and quite unique. The Career Beliefs Inventory (CBI) was created by John Krumboltz in 2005 (see accompanying box for an interview with Krumboltz) and it uncovers values, ideas, and beliefs. The CBI is loosely based on his ideas of happenstance. The concept of happenstance is built on two main ideas: planning is hard to do without experiences, and sometimes we do not have control. The CBI strives to measure assumptions and generalizations people hold concerning work that may be adaptive or maladaptive. The CBI has 96 items on a 5-point Likert scale and 25 subscales with five overarching themes: current situation, happiness, decision influences, changes, and effort. According to Krumboltz, the CBI it is very helpful for transitions, planning, expanding, and choosing a college major.

Interview With John Krumboltz

Figure 13.2 John Krumboltz

This telephone interview took place at 3:00 p.m. on Friday, February 13, 2015. Krumboltz's answers to the questions are summarized and paraphrased.

Q1:   What is the current state of career practice? What is cutting edge?
A1:   The cutting edge is that we do not know in advance what job will be good for us. Therefore, your main aim should be to take action and try different activities. You can volunteer, do pre-internships, internships, job shadowing, and informational interviews. Actually, it is best if you work; really do the work and learn.
Q2:   In this book, we suggest assessing characteristics, skills, and values/interests/beliefs when choosing a career. What do you suggest assessing?
A2:   Assessments can only tell so much. It is a mistake to say assessments tell the whole story. Get a variety of experiences working at different jobs and apprenticeships. I am currently a professor, but I did not start with this job.
Q3:   Besides your own Career Beliefs Inventory (CBI), what assessment do you recommend using?
A3:   Assessment is only part of the picture. Yes, assessments help, but you have to have experiences. Apprenticeships are good. The Strong Interest Inventory Assessment is good. But interests change, though.
Q4:   How did you go about developing the CBI?
A4:   First, I want to say that people have some beliefs that interfere with happiness and some beliefs that lead to happiness and joy. I started out making the CBI by asking people about their career beliefs. I asked, "What is a belief you had that has been validated and true and what is a belief that has proven not to be true?" I also gathered stories and made speeches, keynote speeches. I learned from others about good beliefs and not so good beliefs.
Q5:   Do you have any practical advice to share with someone who is looking for a job in the field of child and adolescent development?
A5:   Have some experience working with children, taking care of children. Do some thinking about relevant activities. Discuss and talk about them with others. Do them. Search for experiences and network.
Q6:   Tell us about your own career, career path, and journey.
A6:   I am a professor, but I had many jobs before that. Are you sure you want to hear all of it? It all started when I was 5 years old and learned to ride a bike in Cedar Rapids, Iowa. My real name is Dwight John Krumboltz and it is the same as my father. I am called "John" by my middle name and my father is called "Dwight." I put "John" on my diploma and passport. Well anyway, I would explore on my bike when I was young, from 5 years on until 7 years. At 7 years old my friend from kindergarten saw me riding and taught me to play ping pong. When we were 11 years old, he taught me to play tennis, but we played it like it was ping pong. One day we went and played on a regulation tennis court and two men saw us. Those two men taught us to play tennis the right way. I played tennis in high school. After high school, I went to Coe College and played on the varsity tennis team. I decided to major in psychology in my sophomore year because my tennis coach suggested it. He was a professor of psychology at Coe College, too, in addition to being coach of tennis. I had received an email stating that I had to declare my major. I took some courses and liked them. Since my coach suggested it, I majored in psychology.

It got to be my senior year and I asked a professor what I should do after I graduate. This professor told me of a fellowship for people from Iowa, to attend

Columbia University in New York. I applied and I got the fellowship. It paid room, board, tuition, transportation, and gave a bit of spending money. At Teacher's College Columbia University, I chose educational psychology with school counseling as a focus. I took classes to learn to teach social studies. I had to take a speech test, but I flunked it. I went to the professor to ask him why I flunked the test. He said it was because I spoke with an accent. I told the professor that he spoke with an accent and not me. The professor then passed me on the speech test.

Meanwhile, I did my practice teaching in the Puerto Rican district of New York and got good experience working with Spanish speakers. After I graduated from the program, I applied for a job in school counseling in the state of Iowa. I sent around 40 letters to different superintendents after graduating and only received responses from about four people. One letter asked me to stop by Waterloo, Iowa and inquire about a job. I found someone to give me a ride to Waterloo, Iowa, as he was going that way. I got a job there as a school counselor in Waterloo and worked there for two years. I joined the Iowa Personnel and Guidance Association and went to a conference in Des Moines, Iowa. Dr. Willis E. Dugan was there as the keynote speaker and he gave a speech. He was from Minnesota. The speech was about the 18 things a school counselor should do. I listened and learned, because I was not doing any of those things. I was doing what I learned at Teacher's College. I listened and reflected. I applied to a summer program in Minneapolis to learn. I took some courses at the University of Minnesota. I had to take a lot of tests and then I got offered a job as a teaching assistant for Willis E. Dugan.

I was torn, because I wanted to return for a third year to Waterloo, Iowa. However, I also wanted to work with Dr. Dugan. I asked another professor in the summer program what to do, he asked me to come back and then asked me to stay. I stayed in Minnesota and became a doctoral student at the University of Minnesota.

While I was there I co-wrote an article on experimental research. It was about shortcuts to experimental research and it was published in a journal. It was only two pages long. My friend and classmate Bill and I wrote it. Bill actually suggested it. This happened the first semester of the first year and faculty were impressed. This leads me to say that unplanned events happen that effect what your career will be. You have to go out and do things because it is the unplanned events.

Then Bill and I did an experimental study about the best way to teach study skills and it was also published. After I graduated from the doctoral program, I served two years in the Air Force. This is because I was in ROTC at Coe College. In the Air Force I did research and published articles for two years. Then Willis E. Dugan got me a job at Michigan State University in the School of Education. Dr. Dugan's friend was dean of the school of education. I spent two years at MSU and then Stanford asked me to apply for a position. I was happy to leave three feet of deep snow. So, I interviewed at Stanford and got hired to do research in Counseling. I got a joint appointment in education and psychology at Stanford to teach counseling and do research. I currently still hold that post.

[These events were unplanned, but they significantly impacted his career.]

Q7:   Any other advice?
A7:   Do things. Try things. Take the Happenstance Approach. Take advantage of unplanned events. Do things to help others and let people know what you are doing. Learn everything you can.

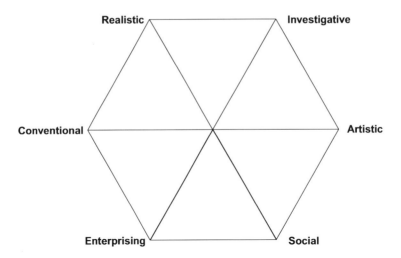

Figure 13.3 Holland's Hexagon

Source: Holland (1997); reproduced by special permission of the publisher.

The Career Key Test

The last test can be categorized as mixed. The Career Key test is also on Holland's theory (Holland, 2014). It is mixed because it measures personality and matches it with work environments that will be suitable and satisfying for the measured personality type. Holland's theory describes six personality types, six matching work environments, and other compatible work environments. The personality types are on a hexagon (see Figure 13.3). Similar personality types and similar work environments are closer to each other on the hexagon. Matching personality types and work environments this way helps people to feel comfortable and be successful at work by using their skills and being themselves.

There exist many career assessment instruments other than those mentioned in this chapter. If you are interested exploring more of them, : *A counselor's guide to career assessment instruments* might be helpful (Wood & Hays, 2013). Again we do not promote any of these assessments, we only offer information that might be useful to you as you continue on your career trajectory.

After Reflecting and Assessing

Now that you have paused and reflected and perhaps taken some formal assessments, what career possibilities seem plausible? In the field of child and adolescent development, a person has options besides teaching children. There are jobs such as recreational therapist, occupational therapist, applied behavioral analyst, policy maker or advocate, family lawyer, and much more. A person in the field of child and adolescent development can have a rich and varied career in any vocational area mentioned in this textbook. In order to find the right one for you, it is important to take in all information and narrow down your choices.

We suggest, on the one hand, narrowing down your choices to three or five vocational areas at first. On the other hand, you may be a person who knows what they want to do at this point. In that case, you have one choice on which to put all your time and energy.

Depending on where you are in your life and your current situation, you may have some difficulty narrowing down your choices to three to five vocational areas. If you are still narrowing your choices at this point, we strongly suggest that you take a standard career assessment or seek some career counseling. You may also want to consult a life coach. A life coach is a professional who helps others with optimizing their lives. Once you have narrowed your choices to one, three, or five, it is time to get some experience. In some cases, it may be more experience and in other cases, it may be new experience.

In general, there are a few types of methods for getting experience. As mentioned in Chapter 14, you can job shadow, volunteer, apprentice, pre-intern, intern, and get paid to get work experience. You can also observe, conduct informational interviews, and network. To network means to get to know and contact people who can help you. All of these experiences help you to learn about the professions you choose to investigate further. It is important to remember Krumbotlz's advice to do something and take advantage of unplanned circumstances. Once you narrow your choices and get some work experience, take steps to enter your chosen profession.

Becoming a Professional

To become a professional, you can seek out any and all information about your chosen career. Continue to keep getting experience that is related and helpful toward your career goal. Create professional portfolios of your work, create resumes, network, contact references, and line up reference letters. All of this information is mentioned in depth in Chapter 14 of this textbook. Do not hesitate to visit the career center at your university or get career advice and counseling from a local life coach. Prepare for interviews in a comprehensive manner. Keep learning about your profession and the company or organization that will be interviewing you. As mentioned in Chapter 14 of this book, you can learn about the company or organization through internet searches, informational interviews, and such. Continue to seek out information and learn. Above all, always be ethical in your career and personal life. Watch your social media presence. Social media presence was discussed in Chapter14, but is worth mentioning here.

The Foundation

The foundation to a career in the field of child and adolescent development is a degree in the field or a related degree. Whether the degree is an Associates or a Doctorate, a degree is your foundation and the knowledge and experience and skills you gain while obtaining it. Additional degrees and experiences may be required depending on what your chosen vocational area and career area. With a degree in child and adolescent development, you have a foundation upon which to build your dreams, happiness, and joy.

Summary

This chapter has taken you on a journey of reflection and preparation in terms of your career. You have taken steps to know yourself better and examined your current situation. You have taken an honest and thorough assessment of your resources in preparation for taking another step in your career. This chapter also took you through the process of setting career goals and creating career plans. This chapter also provided invaluable information about standardized tools for assessing your characteristics, abilities, skills, interests, values, and beliefs in terms of your career. Lastly, this chapter introduced information from

Chapter 14 about taking the steps to become a professional in the field of child and adolescent development. It was our hope that this chapter, indeed this textbook, is a helpful guide to you as you explore and choose a career.

Reflective Questions

1. Who are you really? How well do you and others know who you are?
2. What skills and abilities do you have? What skills and abilities can you learn?
3. What are your true interests and values that motivate you?
4. Of all the careers explored in this textbook, which one is the best fit?

References

Campbell, D. (1992). *Campbell Interest and Skill Inventory*. San Antonio, TX: Pearson Clinical.

CPP. (2004). *Strong Interest Inventory Assessment: Technical Brief*. Palo Alto, CA: Consulting Psychologist Press.

CPP. (2012). *Strong Interest Inventory Assessment: Revised*.

Dembo, M. (2008). *Motivation and learning strategies for college success* (3rd ed.). New York: Erlbaum.

Erikson, E. H. (1963). *Childhood and society* (2nd ed.). New York: Norton.

Erikson, E. H. (1982). *The lifecycle completed: A review*. New York: Norton.

Holland, J. (1997). *Making vocational choices* (3rd ed.). Lutz, FL: Psychological Assessment Resources.

Holland, J. (2014). *Career Key Test*. Raleigh, NC: North Carolina State University.

Johnson, W. (2007). Genetic and environmental influences on behavior: Capturing all the interplay. *Psychological Review*, 114(2), 423–440.

Krumboltz, J. D. (2005). *Career Beliefs Inventory*. Menlo Park, CA: Mind Garden.

Littauer, F., & Littauer, M. (2006). *The personalities*. Ventura, CA: Regal Books.

Myers, I. B. (1962). *The Myers-Briggs type indicator: Manual*. Palo Alto, CA: Consulting Psychologists Press.

Sandoval-Lucero, E., Maes, J. B., & Klingsmith, L. (2014). African-American and Latina(o) community college students' social capital and student success. *College Student Journal*, 48(3), 522–533.

Wood, C., & Hays, D. (Eds.). (2013). *A counselor's guide to career assessment instruments* (6th ed.). Broken Arrow, OK: National Career Development Association.

Chapter 14

Reflections on Career Preparation

Chapter 13 is a reflection on you and choosing a career. This chapter helps you prepare for that career choice. Since you have considered your own personality, values, and preferences in terms of your career, now you can begin preparing for that career and the beginning of an important part of your life. There are many careers and career paths available with a beginning in child and adolescent development. Once you narrow your choice down to one, you can begin preparing to enter that career field.

Job Search Process and Tools

The process for obtaining a job and the tools to use are varied. In this chapter we present some of the more traditional and widely used job search processes and tools. However, please know that there are many possible tools and journeys. This is demonstrated in the career journey interviews in the previous chapters. No matter how your job journey ends, we suggest that after you choose a career you begin your journey with some job observation and research (see Figure 14.1).

During the job observation and research step of the journey, you find out as much as you can about the job by reading, searching databases, searching the internet, and hopefully conducting some nonintrusive and noninteractive observing. This can be done as part of college coursework. For instance, in a professional development, fieldwork, service learning, or capstone course, you can have some observation assignments that offer the opportunity to observe your career of interest. Usually, that observation is accompanied by some type of research. However, the observation and research can be done outside of a class, too. Your local library is a good place to start for research on various careers. You can then ask people who are in your career of interest if you can observe them. This first step is different than job shadowing, because it is not intrusive or interactive.

Ideally, the next step in obtaining a job and becoming employed would consist of two interactive and parallel processes. One process is creating the necessary tools and the other is obtaining more and more experience. As mentioned previously, the process of obtaining a job and beginning a career journey can vary significantly for each person. What we are describing in this chapter is one hypothetical path to obtaining a career and gainful employment. We begin by describing some of the tools you can create or use to aid you in obtaining a job.

Job Search Tools

A portfolio is a collection of items and documents that are relevant to your career preparation (Satterthwaite & D'orsi, 2003). The artifacts validate assertions you make about your career preparation, readiness, and experience. If you want to be a teacher, your portfolio would include a lesson plan. For a professor, it would include a peer-reviewed article. To

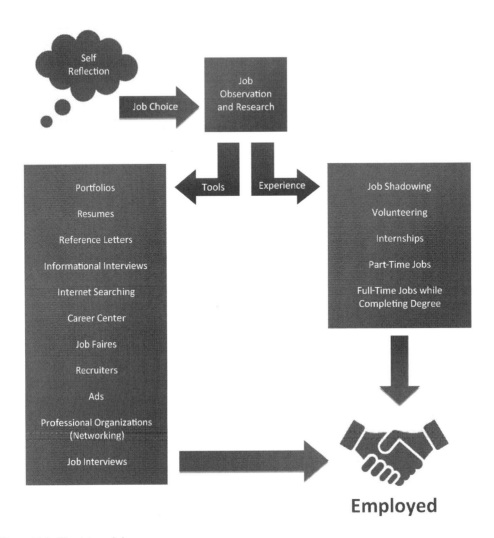

Figure 14.1 Obtaining a Job

work in the nonprofit sector, you might include a winning grant proposal in your portfolio. If behavior analysis is your career of choice, you might include a behavior management plan or chart to demonstrate your competence. Conducting some informational interviews might be helpful in determining what to include in your portfolio (Satterthwaite & D'orsi, 2003). Informational interviews are a means for gathering information about your chosen industry and field (Satterthwaite & D'orsi, 2003). You can also make an electronic portfolio, a website that makes the artifacts and documents readily available and searchable all the time (Whitcomb, 2006).

Résumés basically list information about job preparation and experience. However, résumés can be designed and laid out in a variety of formats, including electronic résumés (Figler, 1999; Whitcomb, 2006). Usually, a résumé is requested at the beginning of the process and can be used to eliminate you from serious consideration. However, Figler (1999) suggests hand-carrying your résumé or in some other way meeting the résumé recipient face-to-face.

This way your résumé is less likely to end up in the circular file with other rejects. There are many types and designs for résumés. We suggest you visit your college's career center or search the internet for résumé formats for the specific job that interests you. If you are looking for more than one type of job, then you should tailor the résumé design and content for each job. For instance, résumés for professor positions and some research positions are called curriculum vitae and do not confirm to the traditional résumé design and length.

Solid and supportive reference letters are other important tools in your arsenal, as you try to find the best fitting job. Anywhere from two to four reference letters are usually required. Be sure that you contact the people providing your references, so that they are not caught off guard and can prepare your letter ahead of the due date. Some employers request that very specific questions are answered on reference forms. Some employers require that both a letter and a form are submitted. References are important, because they aide potential employers in knowing if you can do the job for which you are applying. Usually the letter and form for references are submitted electronically. Also, be fully aware that your potential employer may call your references for additional information.

Another set of tools that can help you learn about a job and secure a job is interviews. There are two basic varieties of interviews: the informational interview and the job interview. The reality is that in today's job search environment, you may be asked to do two, three, or even more job interviews before obtaining a job.

Let us begin by describing informational interviews. To begin with, you must request an informational interview. If it is granted, you arrive in appropriate dress and ask questions to get to know more about the company or organization. A sample question is, "I see from your website that your mission is keeping children together with their biological parents. Can you tell me how that mission informs your day-to-day duties?" You may want to bring a notebook and jot down pertinent information for your job hunt while conducting the informational interview. Please remember that you are not selling yourself, your skills, or your previous experiences. You are merely getting information about a potential employer in order to learn and show some interest.

In contrast, job interviews come toward the end of your climb to obtain a job and they come at the employer's request. This interview may happen after your potential employer reviews a packet of materials. Additionally, there are usually two or three or more job interviews before obtaining a job. Whitcomb (2006) describes the four phases of job interviews: connect, clarify, collaborate, and close. She goes on to refine her process by saying that the behavior exhibited in each phase varies, depending on whether it is a first or a later interview (see Table 14.1). In the first phase, you initiate and create a relationship. In the second phase,

Table 14.1 The Four Cs in First and Subsequent Interviews

	First Interview	Second and Subsequent Interviews
Connect	By initial research, commonalities, respect	By continued research, follow through, respect
Clarify	Big-picture details	Fine-tuning details
Collaborate	Depending on length of interview, surface-level to high-level issues	High-level, confidential issues
Close	Establish agreement about mutual interest; close gaps; convey enthusiasm; ask for the job if there is to be only one interview.	Confirm mutual commitment; close gaps; convey enthusiasm; ask for the job.

Source: Whitcomb (2006), p. 379

you explain why you are appropriate for the position available. In the third phase, you give specifics about how you would perform the job and give examples from similar previous experiences. Lastly, you state your interest in the position and your particular commitment to it. The four phases are the same whether you are in your first or your fifth job interview. In general, you just get more and more specific with in subsequent interviews.

The next tool we want to discuss is the career center at your university or college. If you are not currently in school, you may consult career consultants or private career counselors or coaches to find some of the same information and support. However, we are speaking more directly about career centers that are found on college campuses. Career centers can help you with a wide range of job search tasks. They can assess your personality, values, and preferences in terms of your career. They can give you a place to conduct internet searches and give you sample résumés. They can find volunteer experiences and internship experiences for you, too. They also have career fairs and databases of professional organizations that you may want to join to aid your job hunt. Some career centers even have lists of recruitment companies in the field of child and adolescent development that you can contact during your job search. At some colleges and universities, potential employers post job announcements at career centers and actually come to the campus to conduct interviews. In your sophomore and/or junior year, you should make your initial visit to the career center. In your senior year, you should visit the career center often.

Let us now look a little closer at some of the job hunting tools available at the career center, beginning with internet searches (you can do these on your own, but your career center may have special search engines). Internet searches help you to find out information about a company, people at the company, and specific information about jobs and positions available. Most potential employers have websites just ready for you to discover. You can also search databases of available jobs and sign up for daily or weekly job announcements to be delivered to your email box. Certain websites even allow you to post résumés and network with people in your field or potential employers. According to Dikel and Roehm (2000), everything that was once done "offline" can now be done on the internet (online) in terms of job searching. However, they also suggest that you uncover these three things before you begin an internet search: your skills and interests, your preferred field and employers, and your preferred location (Dikel & Roehm, 2000). Career centers usually help you and support you with all the hardware, software, and human support to conduct internet searches.

The counselors in a career center also plan, arrange, and conduct job fairs. These events are where potential employers come to provide information about their organization, and/or gather résumés, and/or interview potential employees. Sometimes local community organizations also have job fairs. Additionally, alum of a particular college or university may come to an on-campus job fair if they pay a nominal fee. On-campus job fairs are usually held more than one time a year and they can have themes, such as jobs in education or jobs in business or nonprofit organizations. Get to know your career center and the calendar of job fairs that are offered.

Career centers can also help you contact recruiting agencies, find print and online ads, and obtain memberships in relevant professional organizations. Recruiting agencies help potential employers find specific and targeted potential employees, sometimes in large numbers. They also help potential employers with the screening of the applicants. Ads, whether print or online are traditional job announcements and solicitations. These can be useful sometimes, but Figler (1999) reminds us that personal contacts and connections really help. Ads can be included in your job search strategy, but should not be your main tool. Professional organizations are very helpful in obtaining employment. Members are seen to have a certain commitment to their chosen field. The typical college or university career center has lists of professional organizations in the child and adolescent development field. After joining a select number of these organizations, you can network, read targeted job announcements, and be kept abreast of current happenings and trends in the field—all of which can help you obtain relevant, gainful employment.

Gaining Pre-Employment Experience

The job search process and tools mentioned previously in this chapter is quite helpful. However, you also need to acquire some experience with your chosen career in order to be competitive in this job market. This section of the chapter examines various types of methods for getting some job experience. The methods discussed here are job shadowing, volunteering, obtaining an internship, and actual jobs. Let us begin by discussing job shadowing.

Job shadowing is more than just observation and can be your first step toward getting some actual experience. When job shadowing, you are more interactive. You do more than just sit back and take notes. You actively ask questions. You shadow an employed person as he or she participates in all aspects of his or her job for a significant amount of time. This amount of time could be a full week or more. Job shadowing serves as a first step towards learning and getting real experience in the field of child and adolescent development.

Volunteering is another way to experience in the field. Many organizations and businesses in this field allow for volunteers. For example, advocacy groups, nonprofit organizations, educational entities, and medical facilities all welcome volunteers. You get an orientation, some training, and some actual job duties. You are usually required to have regular hours over a substantial amount of time. Some college students volunteer while being educated. This helps them to have a foot in the door of a potential employer. However, look at volunteering as a method of obtaining experience and not a guarantee of a job.

Internships are traditional methods of getting experience and can be paid or unpaid. Paid internships are somewhat like apprenticeships. Internships vary in time commitment from a summer to two or more years. Usually, more responsibility is given to the intern over time. Additionally, internships are usually more regular and structured and purposeful than volunteer experiences. Internships are also more likely to lead to a job than a volunteer experience. You can discover internships through your professors or through the career center. This is why visiting the career center in the sophomore year is desirable.

Working an actual job while going to college is not uncommon. In fact, in the field of child and adolescent development, there are a number of actual jobs you can obtain while in college. For instance, you can work in ECE, in afterschool programs, as a research assistant, as a teaching assistant (in Pre-K through 12 or the college level), as a behavioral technician, or other related fields. You can work part time or full time. We recommend working part-time while obtain your college degrees, because full-time schooling and a full-time job mean a lot of working hours and undue stress. While in college, it is best to focus mostly on your education and learning skills. However, actually working part time in the field can help you gain valuable experiences and see the relevance of some of your coursework and classes and assignments. This experience and learning can help you be prepared for and obtain relevant full-time work that is in the field much sooner upon graduation.

Social Media Presence

In the age of the internet and social media, you must monitor what potential employers can discover about you online. In other words, be careful what you post on social media outlets, such as LinkedIn, Facebook, Snapchat, Instagram, Twitter, and other social media outlets. It is important that you monitor what you post and what friends and others post about you. Just as you use the internet to find out about potential employers, they will use the internet to find out about you.

General Job Ethics

Specific job ethics and standards were shared in previous chapters. Here we want to remind you of some general ethical guidelines and emphasize their importance. One of the basic ethical guidelines is to respect yourself, your co-workers, your students and their families, and your clients and their families. Respecting yourself and others is a basic ethical principle that is very important in the workplace. Another basic guiding ethical principle is confidentiality. When working with children and their families, you must keep their private information confidential and must not share it with anyone. This includes keeping digital information secure from cyber thieves and hackers. There are other basic ethics, such as to not harass your co-workers or those you serve (students or clients), and to always be honest. Be aware of how important it is to behave in an ethical manner while on the job and in your personal life.

Summary

The last chapter of this textbook helped you to reflect on career preparation after having discovered your own characteristics, values, and goals. It discussed job search tools such as résumés, portfolios, and job fairs. It also presented some avenues for obtaining relevant work experience while still in college, including volunteering and working a relevant part-time job. Additionally, this chapter included a section on social media presence and a section on general job ethics. All of the information included herein helps you to reflect and prepare for obtaining a job in the field of child and adolescent development.

Reflective Questions

1. Were you aware of the specifics of the job search process before reading this chapter? What were some of pieces of information gained by reading this chapter?
2. Do you think it is valuable to gain relevant work experience while still in college? How does this experience help you to relate better to and to comprehend more the theories and concepts you are learning in college?
3. Which of the job search tools mentioned in this chapter were new to you? Which job search tools do you want to learn more about? How can you go about learning more about the valuable information presented in this chapter?

References

Dikel, M. R., & Roehm, F. E. (2000). *The guide to Internet job searching.* Chicago, IL: VGM Career Horizons.

Figler, H. (1999). *The complete job search handbook: Everything you need to know to get the job you really want.* New York: Henry Holt and Company.

Satterthwaite, F., & D'orsi, G. (2003). *The career portfolio handbook.* New York: McGraw-Hill.

Whitcomb, S. B. (2006). *Job search magic.* Indianapolis, IN: JIST Publishing, Inc.

Index

Note: Page numbers in italic indicate a figure and page numbers in bold indicate a table on the corresponding page.

AAMFT *see* American Association for Marriage and Family Therapy
AASA *see* American Association of School Administrators
AAUP *see* American Association of University Professors
ACA *see* American Counseling Association
ACLP *see* Association of Child Life Professionals
adoption caseworker 112
AEA *see* American Evaluation Association
American Association for Marriage and Family Therapy 91
American Association of School Administrators 53–54
American Association of University Professors 72, **73**
American Counseling Association 90
American Evaluation Association 62–63
ancillary career options: adoption caseworker 112; career suitability considerations 117; children's librarian 115–116; children's ministry 110–111; family lawyer 111–112; foster care parent 112–113; juvenile justice 112; museum positions 113–115; nanny 109; nonlicensed social work 113; occupational therapy 115; recreational therapy 115; reflective questions 117; summary of themes 100, 116–117
Angel's interview 104–105
applicant characteristics: behavior analyst 94–95, 98, 99; career theory 13, 15, 17; child life specialist 105, 106; children's librarian 116; early childhood education career 30, 32; educational leadership career 50, 52; educational specialist career 61, 62; middle elementary through adult education career 41–44, **42**; museum worker 114–115; nonprofit organizations 79–81; postsecondary careers 68, 69, 71, 72; school counselor 88; *see also* reflection on self

Arnold's interview 70–71
Association of Child Life Professionals 101–103, *102, 103*, 106

BACB *see* Behavior Analyst Certification Board
Bandura, Albert: career theory 12–13; child and adolescent development 4
behavior analyst: Behavior Analyst Certification Board **95**, 95–97, **96**; career path interviews 97–99; career suitability considerations 100; Cherie's interview 97–98; education/certification requirements 94–97, **95**, **96**; ethics 99; ideal applicant characteristics 94–95; job descriptions 94–95; Kristina's interview 98–99; reflective questions 100; salaries 99; summary of themes 100
Behavior Analyst Certification Board **95**, 95–97, **96**; *see also* behavior analyst

Campbell Interest and Skill Survey 129
career areas: ancillary options 109–116; behavior analyst 94–100; counseling based 86–91; education based 21–75, **22**, **23**, **24**, *26*, **30**, **31**; health related 101–107; nonprofit organizations 76–84; *see also* career goals; career preparation reflections; reflection on self
Career Beliefs Inventory 129–131; *see also* career goals
career centers 138–139
career construction theory 12
career goals 126–132, *127, 132*; Campbell Interest and Skill Survey 129; Career Beliefs Inventory 129–131; Career Key Test 132; Myers-Briggs Type Inventory 128; Personalities, The 128; Strong Interest Inventory Assessment 128–129; *see also* career areas; career preparation reflections; reflection on self
Career Key Test 132

career metaphors: action 15; career stories
16–17; cycles 14–15; fit 15; inheritance
14; journey 15; reflective questions 17;
relationships 16; resources 16; roles 15–16;
summary of themes 17; *see also* reflection
on self
career path interviews: Alice's interview
27–28; Angel's interview 104–105; Annette's
interview 29–30; behavior analyst 97–99;
Cherie's interview 97–98; counseling career
87–88; early childhood education careers
27–30; educational leadership career
49–50, 51–52; educational specialist career
59–61, *60, 61*; Erin's interview 105–106;
Frank's interview 110–111; Gary's interview
114–115; Jean's interview 28–29; Kerrie's
interview 87–88; Kristina's interview 98–99;
Lowe, Aisha 82–83; Mallory's interview 49;
middle elementary through adult education
career 41; Mrs. Johnson's interview 41;
museum positions 114–115; nonprofit
organizations 82–83; Nora's interview
51–52; postsecondary careers 67–72; Sally's
interview 116; Sam's interview 89–90; school
psychologist 89–90; Stan's interview 50
career preparation reflections: ethics 140;
gaining pre-employment experience 139; job
search tools 135–139, *136,* **137;** reflective
questions 140; social media presence
139–140; summary of themes 140; *see also*
career goals; reflection on self
career suitability considerations: ancillary
career options 117; behavior analyst 100;
child life specialist career 108; counseling
career 92; early childhood education career
32; educational specialist career 63–64;
middle elementary through adult education
career 40–41, 46; nonprofit organizations
84; postsecondary careers 75; school
psychologist 92
career theory 11–15, *13;* applicant
characteristics 13, 15, 17; Bandura, Albert
12–13; career construction theory 12;
chaos theory of careers 14; Erikson, Erik
14–15; happenstance learning theory 13–14;
John Holland's career theory 13; reflective
questions 17; social cognitive career theory
12–13, *13;* summary of themes 17; systems
theory framework of career development 13
Carl's interview 71–72
chaos theory of careers 14
charter school 37, 38–39
Cherie's interview 97–98
child and adolescent development: application
of developmental theories 8; Bandura, Albert
4; children's rights 5–6; current pedagogy
emphasis 4–6; Dewey, John 4; diversity needs
4–5; education/certification requirements

8–9; Erikson, Erik 4; future directions of
6–7; history of exploitation 3–4; introduction
3–9; Malaguzzi, Loris 4; Montessori,
Maria 4; Piaget, John 4, 6; Preyer, William
3; reflective questions 9; Vygotsky, Lev 4;
Watson, John B. 4
child life specialist: Angel's interview 104–105;
Association of Child Life Professionals
101–103, *102, 103,* 106; career path
interviews 104–106; career suitability
considerations 108; diversity needs 101;
education/certification requirements
101–103, *102, 103,* 104, 105, 107; Erin's
interview 105–106; ethics 106; ideal
applicant characteristics 106; job descriptions
101, 104, 106; reflective questions 107–108;
salaries 106; summary of themes 107
children's librarian 115–116; Sally's interview 116
children's ministry 110–111
children's rights 5–6
CISS *see* Campbell Interest and Skill Survey
cognitive development 8
counseling career: American Association
for Marriage and Family Therapy 91;
American Counseling Association 90; career
path interviews 87–88; career suitability
considerations 92; education/certification
requirements 86–87; ethics 90–91; job
descriptions 86–88; Kerrie's interview 87–88;
reflective questions 92; salaries **91;** summary
of themes 91–92
current pedagogy emphasis: children's rights
5–6; diversity needs 4–5; social justice 5
current situation assessment 123–124, **124;**
see also reflection on self

degree requirements 8–9; child and adolescent
development 8–9
developmental barriers 36–37
developmental milestones 22, 35
developmental strengths 36–37
developmental tasks 35–36
Dewey, John 4
diversity needs: child life specialist 101; current
pedagogy emphasis 4–5; middle elementary
through adult education career 44–45;
nonprofit organizations 79

early childhood education career: Alice's
interview 27–28; Annette's interview
29–30; career path interviews 27–30; career
suitability considerations 32; education/
certification requirements 21–22; ethics 31;
example workdays 24; Head Start programs
26–27, *27;* Jean's interview 28–29; job
descriptions **22,** 22–27, *23, 24, 26;* reflective
questions 32; salaries *30, 31;* summary of
themes 31–32

educational consultant *see* educational specialist career

educational leadership career: career path interviews 49–50, 51–52; career suitability considerations 55; education/certification requirements 48; ethics 53–54; ideal applicant characteristics 52; job descriptions 48, 50–51; Mallory's interview 49; Nora's interview 51–52; reflective questions 55; salaries 52; Stan's interview 50; summary of themes 55

educational specialist career: career path interviews 59–61, *60*, *61*; career suitability considerations 63–64; education/certification requirements 58–59; ethics 62, *62*–63; ideal applicant characteristics 62; job descriptions 57–58, **58**, 59, *60*, *61*; Ralph's interview 61; reflective questions 63; salaries 62; summary of themes 63; Vanessa's interview 59–61

education-based career areas: children's librarian 115–116; counselors 86–88, **91**; early childhood education 21–32, **22**, **23**, *24*, *26*, **30**, **31**; educational leadership 48–55; educational specialist 57–64; middle elementary through adult education 34–46; postsecondary 65–75, **73**, **74**; school psychologist 88–92, **91**

education/certification requirements: behavior analyst 94–97, **95**, **96**; Behavior Analyst Certification Board **95**, 95–97, **96**; child and adolescent development 8–9; child life specialist 101–103, *102*, *103*, 104, 105, 107; counseling career 86–87; early childhood education career 21–22; educational leadership career 48; educational specialist career 58–59; middle elementary through adult education career 39–40; postsecondary careers 66–67; school psychologist 88, 89

emotional development 8

Erikson, Erik: career theory 14–15, 36; child and adolescent development 4

Erin's interview 105–106

ethics: American Association for Marriage and Family Therapy 91; American Association of School Administrators 53–54; American Association of University Professors 72, **73**; American Counseling Association 90; American Evaluation Association 62–63; Association of Child Life Professionals 106; behavior analyst 99; career preparation reflections 140; child life specialist 106; counseling career 90–91; educational leadership career 53–54; educational specialist career 62–63; middle elementary through adult education career 45–46; National Association of School Psychologists 91; National Association of the Education of Young Children 23, 31; National Education

Association 45–46; nonprofit organizations 81–82; postsecondary careers 72, **73**; school psychologist 90–91

examination of resources 125–126, **126**; *see also* reflection on self

family lawyer 111–112, 112–113

foster care parent 112–113

Frank's interview 110–111

gaining pre-employment experience 139

Gary's interview 114–115

happenstance learning theory 13–14

Head Start programs 26–27, *27*

history of child exploitation 3–4

Holland, John 13, 132

interview skills **137**, 137–138

Jesse's interview 67–68

job descriptions: adoption caseworker 112; behavior analyst 94–95; career suitability considerations 117; child life specialist 101, 104, 106; children's librarian 115–116; children's ministry 110–111; counseling career 86–88; early childhood education career **22**, 22–27, **23**, *24*, *26*; educational leadership career 48, 50–51; educational specialist 57–58, **58**, 59, *60*, *61*; family lawyer 111–112; foster care parent 112–113; juvenile justice 112; middle elementary through adult education career 34–35, 37–39; museum positions 113–115; nanny 109; nonlicensed social work 113; nonprofit organizations 76–79; occupational therapy 115; postsecondary careers 65–72; recreational therapy 115; school psychologist 89

job search tools 135–139, **136**, **137**; career centers 138–139; interview skills **137**, 137–138; portfolio preparation 135–136; reference letter 137; résumé 136–137

John Holland's career theory 13

juvenile justice career 112–113

Kerrie's interview 87–88

Kristina's interview 98–99

Krumboltz, John 129–131; *see also* career goals

legal system careers: adoption caseworker 112; family lawyer 111–112; foster care parent 112–113; juvenile justice career 112–113

Littauer, Fred 128; *see also* career goals

Lowe, Aisha 82–83

magnet school 37, 38

Malaguzzi, Loris 4

Mallory's interview 49

marriage, family, and child counselors *see* counseling career

marriage and family therapists *see* counseling career

MBTI *see* Myers-Briggs Type Inventory

MFCC *see* counseling career

MFT *see* counseling career

middle elementary through adult education career: career path interviews 41; career suitability considerations 40–41, 46; charter school 37, 38–39; diversity needs 44–45; education/certification requirements 39–40; ethics 45–46; ideal applicant characteristics 41–44, **42**; job descriptions 34–35, 37–39; magnet school 37, 38; Mrs. Johnson's interview 41; private schools 37, 39; public school 37, 38; reflective questions 46; social justice 45; summary of themes 46; teaching concepts 35–37

Montessori, Maria 4

Mrs. Johnson's interview 41

museum positions: career path interview 114–115; job description 113–114

Myers-Briggs Type Inventory 128

NAEYC *see* National Association of the Education of Young Children

nanny 109

NASP *see* National Association of School Psychologists

National Association of School Psychologists 91

National Association of the Education of Young Children 23, 31

National Education Association 45–46

NEA *see* National Education Association

nonlicensed social work career 113

nonprofit organizations: career path interviews 82–83; career suitability considerations 84; diversity needs 79; education/ certification requirements 76, 82, 83; ethics **81–82**; examples of 78–79; ideal applicant characteristics 79–81, 83; job descriptions 76–79; Lowe, Aisha Dr. interview 82–83; reflective questions 84; salaries **84**; summary of themes 84

Nora's interview 51–52

pediatric dental hygienist 107; *see also* child life specialist

pediatric nurse career 107; *see also* child life specialist

personal goals 127; *see also* reflection on self

Personalities, The 128

physical development 8

Piaget, John 4, 6

portfolio preparation 135–136

postsecondary careers: Arnold's interview 70–71; career path interviews 67–72; career suitability considerations 75; Carl's interview 71–72; education/certification requirements 66–67; ethics 72, **73**; ideal applicant characteristics 68, 69, 71, 72; Jesse's interview 67–68; job descriptions 65–72; reflective questions 74–75; salaries 72–74, **74**; summary of themes 74; Susie's interview 69–70

Preyer, William 4

private schools 37, 39

public schools 37–38

Ralph's interview 61

recreational therapy 115

reflection on self: becoming a professional 133; career goals 126–132, *127*, *132*; current situation assessment 123–124, **124**; examination of resources 125–126, **126**; personal goals 127; reflective questions 134; self-reflection assessment 121–123, **122**; summary of resources 124–125; summary of themes 133–134; *see also* reflective questions

reflective questions: ancillary career options 117; behavior analyst 100; career metaphors 17; career preparation reflections 140; career theory 17; child life specialist 107–108; counseling career 92; early childhood education career 32; educational leadership career 55; educational specialist career 63; middle elementary through adult education career 46; nonprofit organizations 84; postsecondary careers 74–75; reflection on self 134; school psychologist 92; *see also* reflection on self

résumé 136–137

salaries: behavior analyst 99; child life specialist 106; counseling career **91**; early childhood education career *30, 31*; educational leadership career 52; educational specialist career 62; nonprofit organizations **84**; postsecondary careers 72–74, **74**; school psychologist **91**

Sally's interview 116

Sam's interview 89–90

school psychologist career: career path interviews 89–90; career suitability considerations 92; education/certification requirements 88, 89; ethics 90–91; job descriptions 88–89; National Association of School Psychologists 91; reflective questions 92; salaries **91**; Sam's interview 89–90; summary of themes 91–92

self-reflection assessment 121–123, **122**; *see also* reflection on self

self-reflection evaluation *see* reflection on self

SIIA *see* Strong Interest Inventory Assessment

social cognitive career theory 12–13, *13*

social development 8

social justice: current pedagogy emphasis 5; middle elementary through adult education career 45

social media presence 139–140

Stan's interview 50

Strong Interest Inventory Assessment 128–129

summary of resources 124–125; *see also* reflection on self

summary of themes: ancillary career options 116–117; behavior analyst 100; child life specialist 107; counseling career 91–92; early childhood education career 31–32; educational leadership career 55; educational specialist career 63; middle elementary through adult education career 46; nonprofit organizations 84; postsecondary careers 74; reflection on self 133–134; school psychologist 91–92

Susie's interview 69–70

systems theory framework of career development 13

teaching concepts: barriers 36–37; milestones 22, 35; strengths 36–37; tasks 35–36; transactional model 36–37

transactional model 36–37; *see also* teaching concepts

Vanessa's interview 59–61

Vygotsky, Lev 4

Watson, John B. 4